Contents

Acknowledgements

<u>Because manners are very important</u>

About the Author

Helen lives in Greater Manchester with her husband and two children.

Writing lesson plans and resources for teachers by day, Helen is also an author having released her debut book *Cold Coffee* in February 2021, in which she candidly shares her own bumpy journey of becoming a mother. She has also written as a contributing author in *Love Thy Body: Real Life Stories Volume Two*, sharing her story, 'Low Tide', which describes her journey from self-loathing to self-love and her recovery from mental trauma, due for release at the end of February 2021.

Following her experience with postnatal depression and maternal mental health, Helen is an avid supporter of normalising the subject and breaking stigmas attached to this by speaking out honestly and openly, whilst attempting to educate, encourage and empower the community with a touch of humour through her words. She wings her way through life and parenting with her mantra "This too shall pass" and the support of some good quality gin.

To contact Helen, please follow her social media pages:

Facebook: https://www.facebook.com/coldcoffee34

Instagram: https://instagram.com/cold_coffee85?igshid=jpq6h222lfr2nd

Foreword

Nobody ever asks me what I miss about life before becoming a parent. If they did, I would tell them this:

Sunday mornings used to be about waking up when my mind and body were ready. My eyes would gradually open and I would stay in the warmth and security of my bed, maybe flicking through social media, or thinking about the day ahead, or occasionally judging the damage I had caused myself by consuming one too many drinks the previous evening, until I felt ready to stretch, sit up and move slowly. I'd go for a pee and put my slippers on, then mosey on down to the kitchen to fill the kettle before settling down to watch Sunday Kitchen, interrupted only by the need for more tea, the call of a bacon sandwich or light conversation with the other half. It would be midday before I chose to shower and start my day, well rested and chilled out as Sundays should be – a day of rest.

This pre-parent me would occasionally look forward to future Sundays when I would one day have children. I was sure without doubt that we would fit the image of the family snuggled up together in a beautiful, Egyptian cotton-clad, super-king-sized bed, reading books and watching old school Sunday morning cartoons whilst eating croissants and drinking smoothies or freshly brewed coffee. We would all be laughing and relaxing together, spending quality family time and enjoying each other's company.

The actual reality of Sunday mornings with children hits me weekly like a wet flannel being tossed into my face. I am awoken at an ungodly hour – at least three hours earlier than fresh-faced and well-rested, non-parent me – by the sound of a baby behind bars, screeching for freedom and milk. No more coming around gently, scrolling social media or spending time reflecting on that lovely dream I just enjoyed in which Cillian Murphy was running me a bath. I am shot out of the water cannon straight into the circus ring. Woe betide me should I ignore the cries of the little man, allowing him to escalate and then stir his sleeping (for now) older sibling. No time for a wee, I sit bolt upright straight away, knee joints cracking as I stand up and shove on my old cardigan, which is now used as a stand-in dressing gown, because it has pockets big enough to hold many snotty tissues produced by morning child-phlegm.

Baby retrieved from the prison cell, it's downstairs to make a brew and a bottle (sadly not gin o'clock yet, just his milk time) before nappy change, by which point I still haven't even managed to get to the toilet to relieve myself yet. Then it's time for a string of loud, colourful, cheerful characters on the telly singing songs as the toy box I tidied and sorted through the evening before, is turned over and its contents strewn across the floor. If I dare to leave the room, I'm reminded by said baby that I am in fact pulling too tightly on the imaginary string that he thinks bonds our beings together for all eternity, so that we must never be more than a metre apart.

Then, Number One wakes up. Upon occasion, I'm woken from my slumber by the intense feeling that I'm being watched. I open my eyes drearily to a shadow of bed head – a bit like a burst mattress – inches from my face and the aroma of morning breath finding its way directly into my nostrils. However, she usually stays asleep until she hears movement downstairs and leaps from her bed like a Disney Princess singing with the birds and with the revitalised energy of the battery bunny. Door flung open, she then begins to talk at me (which consequently lasts for the whole duration of the day now that nap times are no longer a thing for her). I gulp my now-cold tea and long for the days of Sunday Kitchen and bacon whilst attempting to pour cereal into bowls and wonder when I'll get a few minutes to pee. It's loud. And busy. And relentless. Right from the moment my eyes are forced open.

Nothing can prepare you for becoming a parent. Literally, nothing. You can watch all the shows, read all the books, listen to all the podcasts, observe friends and family members embark on parenting journeys and still, I guarantee, your understanding will still not even come close to what it actually feels like. One day, you're just doing you, then the next you're suddenly responsible for the growth, development, nurture and happiness of another human being. To some this is a welcome prospect, to others it is frighteningly overwhelming, and to most it's an adjustment that you have to adapt to. Whichever category you fall into, it's okay Your thoughts and feelings are okay, regardless of positivity, negativity, or just plain WTF.

When I first decided to write this book, it was a form of therapy; a way of recording my thoughts and telling myself that winging it was getting me somewhere. But as time went on and my challenges evolved, it became more than that. It is my confirmation that I am normal, my kids are normal(ish), my marriage is normal, my life is normal, and I am not the only one feeling the way I do. There are a number of extremely witty, well-written books on the shelves by women I adore who talk candidly about the hardships and the joys of parenting. Let's not forget the beautifully brave and honest women on social media apps who post regular anecdotes of parenting mishaps, which to be frank, make me howl with laughter and nod my head as I open the gin bottle in solidarity, but few seem to go raw. Sure, they talk of embarrassing incidents and caption those hilarious moments most parents can relate to, yet I can't help but feel there are very few parents who actually say it exactly like it is, warts and all. Brutal honesty. Unashamed admittance. Not sugar-coated just because that's what society expects from us.

Parenting is in fact like Fight Club. There are so many aspects that we aren't supposed to talk about for fear of coming across as vulgar, unempathetic or generally useless. Consequently, there are loads of things nobody tells you about pregnancy, birth and parenting, making it all a massive shock when the time comes. Why not prepare one another properly? Why not speak as you find and not give a fuck about the judgement you might or might not get from someone else just because they had a different experience to yours?

My friends will tell you I'm an over-sharer. I don't think twice about voicing gory details or texting them when something immensely cringe-worthy happens. I enjoy sharing every detail in great description, and I love it when fellow over-sharers do the same to me. Not into TMI? Then this isn't the book for you. My Nana used to call it "girly chat"– the kind of conversations that these days we now have over a group WhatsApp with our Squad in which we know we are free from judgement, comfortable to say anything, and likely to get a variety of useful opinions, advice or just LOLs and camaraderie in return. Back in Nana's day, these Squad chats over a brew in their neighbour's kitchen were a crucial lifeline to females, be they parents or not. The phrase "It takes a village to raise a child" is loosely based on the concept of acknowledgement that women, specifically mothers, need support, be that physical or mental. Parenting is hard and relentless.

So, in an age where we have so many platforms to discuss the details and bring to light the truths, why are there still so many parents feeling isolated, embarrassed or defeated? In my opinion it is because of society's expectations that we should never ask too many questions. We shouldn't speak about the things that might scare or gross out others. We should offer our opinions only when they are asked for, and even then, in a gentle, politically correct way so as not to offend anyone. People are offended far too easily these days. We really ought to get a grip. As long as what you say is kind, helpful, sensitive to the receiver and delivered with good intent, what's the problem? I tell you now, if someone had told me straight up when I was pregnant that there was a high chance I was going to shit myself during delivery, it would've saved me a whole lot of stress and embarrassment at a time when my thoughts really should have been elsewhere. I refuse to believe that I am the only one who feels this way. Surely, I am not alone in thinking that a tad more honesty and reality in a world infected by fake news and secrecy can only be a good thing?

So here I am with my unfiltered, unapologetic and hopefully inspiring story of truth. I don't mince my words. I'm not shy or embarrassed and I'm an open book for all.

Disclaimer: This is NOT a self-help book. This is NOT a parenting guide (I am utterly clueless from one day to the next and am not certified to give any advice other than gin and an early night), and I am certainly NOT medically certified to diagnose any symptoms or ailments other than the fact I myself am slightly unhinged due to one hell of a four-year rollercoaster. This is simply my wonderfully difficult, breathtakingly marvellous, insanely intense, completely honest, bloody bonkers journey into parenthood so far.

1.

Pregnancy

Two pink lines

When I first found out I was pregnant, I was twenty years old. I was living my best life heading towards the end of my second year at university and had been with my boyfriend for about three months. Browsing the aisles at Boots with a friend, I suddenly felt compelled to buy a pregnancy test – something I hadn't ever considered until that moment – but as I stood there looking at them, it dawned on me that I couldn't remember when I'd had my last period. As a stereotypical student who frequented the pub, ate frozen crispy pancakes for breakfast and spent my student loan in the Topshop sale, I honestly did not think I was pregnant. Test purchased, we went home to my student flat and I did the test. Two very bright pink lines appeared. Shit. All I remember about the 24 hours which followed were smoking a full packet of No.1s, a lot of crying and the utter dread that I had to go home and tell my mum. I already knew I didn't want to keep the baby. To make things more interesting, picture the timing of the incident: I was in the midst of a dancing show in which costumes included sequin crop tops and lycra leotards – not exactly ideal for concealing a secret bump under the most unforgiving, fluorescent stage lighting in front of a packed-out audience – but timing has never been my forte! Anyone who has participated in amateur dramatics or dancing as a teen and young adult will know that peers love a gossip! So, I ploughed through two weeks' worth of Can-Can and ballet routines with sudden morning sickness and zero energy, to get to the other side, which for me was a termination.

Why does morning sickness only seem to kick in after you physically see confirmation that you're pregnant?! The first hint of it I experienced was eating a strawberry milk lolly. They still turn my stomach now, although following that, all I wanted to eat were those strawberry jelly sweets. My boyfriend and mum were incredibly supportive throughout the whole thing. She took me to a private clinic where I was met leaving the car by a handful of protesters with banners and candles, telling me I was going to hell.

Nothing like a dedicated protester preaching the opposite of what you're about to go through to put you at ease, eh?! I found out I was nine weeks along. I didn't want to see or know anything else. Just give me the drugs and get me out of there. In hindsight, at twenty years old, I was so naïve to not research further beforehand, but to this day I still don't regret the decision. I took the tablets, read Harry Potter with a curtain closed around my bed, and waited until I could go home. Beyond the privacy of my curtain, I remember hearing women crying and moaning with pain. I was lucky and never felt a thing, but I do remember passing the embryo the next day and the sorrow that accompanied it. Despite having never regretted the decision, I'd be lying if I said I hadn't thought about what might have been on more than one occasion. A medium recently told me that she saw a spirit of the most vivid blue colour calling me Mother. It was such a colour because this represents the purest of spirits, untouched by the human world. She said that this spirit was that child which I never birthed, and that she was my two living children's guardian angel. Comforting and forgiving all in one breath.

The months that followed the termination led to a mild mental breakdown. I went off the rails a tad and broke up with said boyfriend. I pissed off a lot of friends, got dangerously drunk more than once and deferred my university year so I didn't have to sit exams. I spent a few days lying in my uni bedroom with a 24-bag multipack of crisps and a 16-pack of Penguin biscuits for survival. But somewhere along the journey, I snapped back to reality and screwed my head back on and my twenties reclaimed its glory.

Oh God, my twenties. What a glorious time to be alive! Collagen, tanned, toned, selfishly indulgent, the ability to drink all night and go into work on two hours sleep with no hangover. In my thirties, I only have to sniff beer number three now and I'm hungover for a week.

Fast forward nine years to our honeymoon. The boyfriend from the previous encounter turned out to be a very brave and very loyal guy. Having got back together a few months after my breakdown, we got married at 28.

Mr I is a keeper. We'd done practically a decade together, bought a dog, matured through our sublime twenties, got hitched, had a lovely home together and both held down good jobs. The next milestone was obvious. We had spoken about having kids one day and agreed it was something we both wanted.

We waited a year after getting married to go on our honeymoon to Florida.

It was a dream trip, and we knew we had to make the most of it, so there we were on night six, a couple of buckets of Buds deep in a sports bar watching poker on the big screen and having a bloody good laugh. Naturally, one thing led to another and we ended up back in the hotel room about to have sex. I have no clue whose idea it was, or how the conversation went down, but we decided not to use any contraception and got to it. Well, let me tell you, drunken honeymoon sex might be delightful, but waking up the next morning to the realisation that you were both steaming and fully regret the absence of sense to wear a rain mac is enough to sober you up like a kick in the fanny. We absolutely shit ourselves. I swear, after initially laughing it off, we couldn't look one another in the eyes for the entire day! That evening we laughed, agreed we weren't quite ready for parenthood (but if the seed had already been sewn it would be fine), ordered another a bucket of beers and put the box of condoms next to the bed next to the housekeeping tip for all honeymoon bangs to follow.

When honeymoon sex didn't turn into a baby, it didn't take us long upon returning home to change our minds and start trying properly. I remember telling a handful of friends that it was next on the cards for us. It took about eight months of ovulation apps, rampant sex with legs up in the air afterwards and disappointment at each period for me to finally get pregnant, by which time I'd stopped stressing about it and just decided to chill the fuck out and let nature do its thing. So, when I went on a good friend's hen party, I threw caution to the wind when I got a negative result from a very cheap test I'd bought online before drinking commenced, just to make sure. (It was a boozy weekend from start to finish to the point that I woke up fully clothed, including stilettos, on top of the bed on the second morning. Damn Jägerbombs!) I didn't notice that I looked slightly bloated in the size eight fitted dress I'd bought two weeks earlier and dismissed the weird occasional shooting pain in my boobs as a pulled muscle from the gym. Four days later, when my period still hadn't arrived, I became very suspicious and bought a pregnancy test. I took it before jumping in the shower one morning when getting ready for work whilst Mr I was still in bed. Honestly, it was the quickest I have ever showered before having kids. Post-kids showers are now rapid for a variety of reasons, covering everything from the fear of a baby falling off the bed (a parental rite of passage), to the sound of something expensive being broken, or a small child shouting they've done a poo and tried to clean themselves. Nothing gets you out of the shower faster than the latter.

Anyway, this particular speedy wash resulted in a different kind of shock – two blue lines and 3-4 weeks flashing at me. OH MY GOD. Ladies and gentlemen... Game changer. That was the very moment that my life completely altered course. The pinnacle of adulthood. Fuck...The jägerbombs! Enter immediate panic that one wild night might have completely damaged my baby. I was already a terrible parent. I remember running back into the bedroom to tell my half-asleep husband, laughing and crying with excitement, then heading off to work in my floatiest dress, convinced that a positive test meant I now looked six months pregnant and everyone would guess immediately.

The first trimester was good. Other than the achy boobs, the first symptom I noticed was a heightened sense of smell – the air freshener in my car being the initial culprit. Before kids, I was pretty anal about keeping my car immaculate (these days it looks like squatters have just been evicted from the back seats and footwells), so there was always a jazzy scent hanging from the mirror until one morning when I began my commute to work and felt a sudden urge to vomit at the scent in there. When choosing a car freshener now, I still can't bring myself to sniff the new car scent. I was lucky with morning sickness and seemed to dodge it, apart from one morning whilst getting ready for work when I ran to the loo to vomit and wet myself at the same time. And that was before my pelvic floor was destroyed from birthing.

With the first trimester came the first scan, earlier than expected at around seven weeks because I'd had a tiny bit of bleeding. It doesn't matter how chilled and calm you are as a person, there is a pang of anxiety that you cannot avoid when en-route to a baby scan. The obvious worries, panic & questions race through your mind until you get the-all clear. Thankfully, this scan showed that everything was healthy and growing as it should have been, although at that point, there really wasn't much to see on the screen. The second scan at twelve weeks (the dating scan) was far more exciting. As Mr I and I watched the screen, we could see baby in all its developing glory. A surreal but wonderful experience. Such a blessing indeed. My heart absolutely breaks for expectant parents who don't get to feel what we felt that day. I'll also say at this point that I had never seen so much blood exit my body via needle as I did when I was pregnant! (This obviously changed after

I gave birth.) Although I'm not a huge fan of needles, I'm not one to pass out by looking at them. However, I swear that despite being a low-risk pregnancy and generally healthy, it felt like there was a vial of blood required at every appointment! My arm bruised quite badly after each extraction. That said, my community midwife, Amy, was bloody amazing and also pregnant, so I loved her immediately. She will make another poignant appearance later in this book.

Then it was time to announce. A few days after the dating scan, we were attending the wedding of two close friends; an event in which there was no way I could go sober without being clocked. My friends will tell you I am partial to a gin or three. We told close friends beforehand (family already knew from early on in the pregnancy) but decided to keep it off social media until after the wedding.

The Second trimester came around quickly and brought with it weird cravings of tomato soup. Cans and cans of the stuff, to the point I used to carry a can around in my handbag, just in case I needed it! At around eighteen weeks, that craving changed to donuts, and because it was my first baby, I thought sod it; eat all the donuts! I didn't think twice about wanting to lose the weight I was piling on – all three stone of it by the end of the pregnancy!

So, here's a pregnancy symptom nobody tells you about – discharge. When you're actively trying to conceive, you become more aware of this joy based on trying to time ovulation, but honestly, I was not prepared for this. Hormones meant that I produced loads of the stuff; enough to need pantyliners every day for about five months. My constantly padded fanjo was not happy.

The most notable symptom during trimester two was the backache. It began around eighteen weeks and gradually got worse, to the point my hips would lock and I would get a sciatic type pain from my right bum cheek down my thigh. Being 5'4" and a size 6-8 before conception, it goes without saying that I struggled with the weight of the growing bump. Eventually, I was signed off work at twenty-six weeks after a mild breakdown in front of my GP. I was welling up in the waiting room before I even got into her room because I was just so fed up with being in pain. Thus followed the rest of the pregnancy laid up on the couch – very dangerous for the bank account of a first-time parent with online shopping apps and a list of essentials (which you categorically do not need all of, but will insist that you do), second only to online shopping during the night feeds!

Sex was not a priority after this, poor husband. Between discharge, a bad back, a growing bump and the fact I couldn't bend to shave my legs or vaj (or even see them at all towards the end), my minky was firmly off limits. This was totally different in my next pregnancy, but we'll get to that later.

We decided to find out the gender of the baby at the twenty-week scan after we both felt certain it was a boy...it was not! A healthy baby girl was growing in there. At the time, I was working in a primary school before I was signed off, and one of the children used to ask me daily if it was "a Janet or a Jeff", which amused me greatly. Being surrounded by young children when you're pregnant is tiring but great; they share your enthusiasm and ask totally unfiltered questions, "Does Mr I know you're having a baby?" "Are you going to feed it with your boobs?" "Can I come and see it?" They are hilarious!

Along came third trimester and I said *adios* to my feet. I felt like a whale; I was bored, sore, huge, emotional and impatient. Knowing only my sister and two other friends who had had children, I didn't really have anyone other than them to speak to or ask questions. My sister told me that there are certain things about pregnancy and birth that parents do not discuss with non-parents. There is an unspoken rule, apparently to protect non-suspecting mothers-to-be and women who haven't considered having a baby yet. They have to wait until they join the club. Fuck that! Tell them the truth! Although I felt most of my questions at the time were answered honestly, admittedly there were things I didn't ask because I was too embarrassed to share (hello discharge).

The remainder of the pregnancy was fairly uneventful and filled with excitement and naïvety at the epic changes that were literally just around the corner. At around 36 weeks, we finally chose a name for our baby girl – Harriet Esme – which would later evolve to her nickname 'Hurricane Harriet', because the child has a tendency to move at over 100mph and destroy whatever is in her path.

Ding-ding, round Two! Fast-forward twenty-one months and the subject of baby number two crept into conversation. The Terrible Twos hadn't really started by that point, so we were blissfully unaware that our darling charismatic toddler was about to turn into an argumentative, strong willed, stubborn-as-fuck mini 21-year-old with the ability to make us hide in the downstairs toilet eating chocolate just for five minutes respite from trying to reason with her. What kind of nobheads were we when we made the automatic assumption that just because she took eight months to conceive, it would take the same for baby number two, thus leaving us plenty of time to nurture and dismiss the Twos that were brewing inside of her? Massive, ignorant nobheads! Six weeks it took. I think we only had sex about three times. Poor Ste was excited for months of sex on tap, only to be informed after a few weeks that my sexy shop was closed for business for the foreseeable. We got the positive test result a few days before Christmas which told us 1-2 weeks, so we decided to deliver close friends and family the news with a photo of the test inside their Christmas cards, because nothing says happy festive season to the ones you love like a picture of pee on a stick. The best reaction came from my mother-in-law, who thought it was a picture of a pen until she put her readers on and expressed her delight. My own mother had a slightly more subdued reaction as she smiled, congratulated us, then disappeared off into the kitchen to carve the turkey. She would later inform me that she did this because her first thought was that she "knew what was coming" and that I was "going to struggle with the two-and-a-half-year age gap".

So here we go again with another first trimester. Despite knowing that no two pregnancies are the same, I was surprised at how different it was. I felt relentlessly sick until about week eleven, to the point that the GP prescribed anti-sickness tablets to take the edge off, although there was never any actual vomit produced. We were having a new bathroom fitted at the time, and I remember making bacon butties for the lads and just heaving at the smell that once would have made me salivate. Tiredness and exhaustion got to me on a daily basis, but I put this down to parenting a two-year-old as well as hormones. Craving wise, I yearned for white bread and fresh tomatoes, but after having to shift three stone after my first pregnancy, I was careful with the donut intake.

It wasn't until around the halfway mark that I noticed my mood shifting. I was snappy and impatient and was finding it increasingly harder to maintain my standard of parenting with Harriet. Luckily for me, I have a wonderful husband who was happy to take charge of the minion when he wasn't out at work and the weather was kind that Spring, so there were plenty of opportunities for him to take her out to the local park to give me a break. But that was when the guilt slowly crept in. Guilt, unpredictable mood swings, rage, exhaustion, little desire to nest or buy things for the baby or even talk about it. I was completely unaware until many months later that I was experiencing the unwelcome manifestation of antenatal depression during my pregnancy. I didn't even know that such a condition existed. Even the gender scan that told us we were having a healthy baby boy wasn't enough to shake me out of my funk, although Ste was immensely chuffed that he was getting a little Tiger Woods, being a golfer and all. I struggled on like this into my third trimester, telling nobody, with absolutely no admittance to myself that something not right was happening to my brain. I was just blinkered to it all and trying my best to crack on regardless, just as I thought everyone else was doing. I was actually on auto-pilot and the days felt so long, but the weeks flew by. It's only now in hindsight that I can see how poorly I became and how much I wish that I'd recognised it and said something to someone. Prior to my second pregnancy, I had always been the voice of positivity. I was the annoying friend who told people "Everything happens for a reason" and "You get back what you put out there"; words that I had previously lived by and strongly believed, but useless to a person in a black hole who needed more than just words.

Libido during my second pregnancy was completely different to my first. I was one horny housewife. After the initial sickness passed, my sex drive returned in droves, albeit it would peak at annoying times of the day whilst Ste was in work. I wanked like a fourteen-year-old almost daily for about a month until my bump got so big that I couldn't reach my fanny. One evening at 38 weeks pregnant, I announced to my surprised husband that it was his duty to let me mount him and attempt to get things moving. Being a man and all, he didn't hesitate, so we got to it as best we could manage. As good as it felt, it was like a HIIT session; both of us were trying to manoeuvre our way around the kettle bell attached to my stomach to find the good bits, with me wondering that if I just leaned forwards a tiny bit more would I squash his diaphragm and render him unable to breathe. Could I actually kill him during sex here, like a praying mantis? Then all of a sudden, at that euphoric moment as we both reached climax together, I sneezed. Then farted. With him still inside me and coming. I swear, I have never burst into laughter so hard in my life. So hard in fact, that I pissed myself. Yes, whilst he was still inside me, lying on his back between my thighs, completely trapped underneath my weight as my pelvic floor (battered from the first delivery) failed me on an unprecedented level. He hadn't banked on a golden shower. Neither had I. Luckily, he has a sense of humour and we have been together long enough for him to see the funny side. Although, to this day, I'm still not convinced that his tears were from laughter and not utter dismay.

Heavy pregnancy brought the return of severe back ache, so when my community midwife recommended acupuncture to try and curb it, I was very much game. Holistic therapies have always been right up my street, yet I'd never tried this. One sunny afternoon, I arrived at the maternity ward at the hospital, sat in the waiting room amongst all the other expectant ladies, wondering what their stories were, and waited for my name to be called. Imagine my utter delight when the midwife who came to get me was the beautiful soul, Amy, my community midwife during my pregnancy with Harriet, whom I'd liked so much. Feeling at ease because I knew I was in good hands, we chatted away for the hour and I didn't even feel her stabbing me with a thousand tiny needles. After about three weekly sessions, my back felt so much better, but I pretended I still needed the acupuncture therapy because I loved Amy's company so much. Yes, I sound like a sad sap and possibly a little stalkerish, but truth be told, I didn't have many people to talk to who understood this pregnancy and parenting lark, and she made me feel so at ease. As I approached my final month, she told me that the therapy was actually very good for inducing labour and I remember begging her on a weekly basis to get that boy out of my belly, until she relented five days before my due date. It was the hottest summer the UK had seen since the 1970s and I'd spent most of it naked in my house in front of an electric fan with an iced bottle of water on my feet. I felt like a heavy, bored, sweaty hot mess and I was so done with being pregnant. I hated it. Both times. Obviously, I know how lucky I was to have been able to conceive and carry healthy children, but you feel as though you can't actually admit you hate pregnancy because there are so many unfortunate ladies out there who would kill to feel its power. Without wanting to sound ungrateful, pregnancy really was not enjoyable for me. "You're glowing," people would say. "It's sweat and highlighter," I would respond. A dear friend once told me that as she sat in her maternity gown waiting for her c-section at 40 weeks, she turned to her husband and asked him if she had her pregnancy glow yet. I can't remember his response, but I hope he was smart enough to tell her she looked fit in that moment. Anyway, there I was at 39+2, lying on my back like an upside-down hairy turtle, as Amy did a quick check to see what my cervix was up to before she administered the acupuncture needles. Her head popped up between my thighs with a puzzled and slightly surprised expression (my first thought was 'God I knew I should've tried to shave, even my midwife is judging my lady jungle'), and she asked if I had had any twinges at all that day. I replied that I had experienced absolutely nothing, before she announced I was around 4-5cms dilated and she couldn't believe I wasn't experiencing labour pains. Holy fuck. What now? Eh? This baby was on his way and I hadn't even realised. During a previous session I had already asked Amy if she would be my midwife during the birth and deliver baby number two. I trusted her that much I desperately wanted her to be the one to do that. She did the acupuncture, pinned a tissue with some funky smelling oil on it onto my top and told me she would see me in a few hours and to call her when contractions started. Given my short labour with Harriet, in my head it was entirely possible that this one would slip out on our newly renovated bathroom floor tiles with Ste catching him line-backer style, so I left feeling relieved my pregnancy experience would soon be over but shitting myself that I wasn't going to have time to get back to the hospital. Number Two, Teddy Arthur, was on his way.

It's easy for me to sit here now knowing that my pregnancy journey is over – and I categorically will not be doing it again – and say that each of those nine-month periods of my life flew by. But, in retrospect, they didn't. The first twelve weeks of hiding a pregnancy drags as you try to be inventive with your excuses and wardrobe, leading prying eyes and ears off the track and thinking of reasons to dodge people who might guess why you're wearing a long floaty scarf over your midriff before you're ready to reveal. Then you have the tense build-up to the first scan which makes the weeks between the positive result and the ultrasound seem painfully stretched as you find yourself mulling over the future and wondering if baby is okay, as well as getting your head around the fact that you are now carrying another human inside you. It's a massive awakening for both your mind and your body as hormones rage through you and skin begins to stretch into new shapes. My skin became so dry in my first pregnancy, it just fell off me like a shedding snake, which I found weird given how much water I drank. The second trimester does usually seem to pass more quickly, but as you approach the due date in your third and you are forced to slow down, so to do the weeks. Many ladies miss their bumps once they're gone, but many also welcome back the ability to control their own body to a degree (childbirth robs you of control of a few things, but let's talk about that later). Personally, I was glad to see my feet again and to be able to shave my fanny without standing in front of a mirror, one leg up on the bed and a sheet underneath me to catch falling debris. Or worse, having my husband do it with his electric beard trimmer. That was a low point, although credit to Ste, he did a neat job.

Ailments aside, pregnancy can and should be a wondrous time. Bottom line is that you have created a life. That one sperm found your one egg and they fused to make a life which is growing inside you. Girls, our bodies are remarkable. If pregnancy and birth doesn't make you see that, then I don't know what will. Your body produces hormones that make your pelvis literally soften so that you can push a baby out of it. Your womb is a home for nine months. Everything you eat provides nutrition for someone else inside you. All of your energy is sapped because baby needs it to grow by inches each month. If you're ill, tough, because baby needs those blood cells. Your bladder becomes baby's own yoga ball to bounce on day and night. Your organs are moved about and shoved into different places to make room for a growing baby. Your joints and muscles are required to carry such a weight which lies on your abdomen for weeks and there is no resting stop like a set at the gym. You don't belong to you anymore. You belong to them. You're their bitch from day one. And as hard and tiring as it can be to deal with that, you accept it because it's what you have to do for the end result. And also because you know that for every complaint you make, there is another woman out there who would strike a deal with the devil to be in your shoes, healthy pregnant mamma.

But I do get it. You don't want insomnia. You don't want to get up in the night for a wee three times. You don't want to vomit brushing your teeth. You don't want to cry at a McDonalds advert. You don't want to stand on swollen feet with a sore back. You don't want a hairy bush. You don't want discharge. You don't want indigestion after a family sized bar of chocolate. You don't want constipation. You don't want to move. And you don't want to be told "Well, that's the way it is, you'll get there soon" for nine whole months.

But remember, it's okay to not always enjoy being pregnant, as long as you appreciate the magic that's happening on the inside.

2.

Birth

Ring of fire

Labour with Harriet began on a Tuesday evening, eleven days after my due date, after three sweeps (I had begged the community midwife for the third), and with an induction booked in for two days later, I remember it vividly.

As every first-time mother does, I had spent the previous two weeks bouncing on the yoga ball, eating fresh pineapple and hot curries, taking long hot baths and doing all the things you are told to do to help shift that baby into lock and load position, with the exception of sex (I just couldn't get the thought of my unborn daughter seeing her Dad's penis popping up and down towards her with absolutely no effect). There had been zero P in V action for approximately four months prior to bursting point and I had had absolutely no urges for an orgasm throughout my entire pregnancy. So, when I thought I felt a few very mild flutters, I was surprised. I had expected labour pains to kick in full throttle from the beginning, just like you see on the telly (cramping and squirming and moaning), but these felt kind and gentle. Ste was on his way out to work for the evening, so I told him I'd be fine and I'd just time the feelings and let him know if anything geared up. When he returned home a few hours later, I was fairly sure that whatever I had felt had stopped and I had imagined the whole thing, given my expectations that even early labour pains would have been enough to have me bent double on the floor.

We went to bed and I woke for the toilet at midnight, the first of around three nightly wee breaks since the second trimester. It wasn't unusual, albeit annoying that I hadn't slept through the night for a couple of months. It's true. Pregnancy really does prepare you for parenthood. I now haven't slept through the night for about four years since experiencing insomnia throughout both pregnancies, followed by the inevitably crap baby sleep cycles. Glancing into the toilet after I had finished (as you do automatically when you are pregnant, I don't know why, as I'd never felt the urge to inspect my urine prior to pregnancy but did it every time throughout like I was security examining a liquid at the airport), I noticed a small pinky-white lump of something sitting at the bottom with flecks of blood – my plug. Excited to over-share my findings with Ste, I woke him up and declared that even though I wasn't having contractions, I was going to phone the maternity unit at the hospital just to mention I'd lost my plug after having those flutters earlier on. Leaving him in bed (and almost immediately back to sleep I might add), I went downstairs and made the call.

They were having a quiet night and given I was eleven days past my due date, they said I could nip in for an examination if I wanted to. Too right I did! Not the most patient at the best of times, I wanted to know if anything was happening, so I made Ste get up and dressed and put the hospital bag in the boot of the car. We genuinely thought it wouldn't be needed and we were going to be back home in a couple of hours after a bit of poking and prodding. And then it hit me. I gripped onto the banister at the top of the stairs for support. They say contractions are like waves of cramp-like pains that ebb and flow as your muscles tighten then relax. A wave, my fucking arse. I felt like my arsehole was about to fall out. The best way I can describe it, was like a mixture of the most intense period pain I'd ever had, combined with the kind of cramp you get from food poisoning just before you're about to explode the dodgy prawns you ate from your bowels, multiplied by a hundred, alongside cold sweat and jelly legs. Except this cramp was much lower down in my abdomen and it rendered me absolutely helpless for the duration. You are unable to move whilst it's happening. You just freeze in whatever position you're in, slightly bent over. It feels like someone is squeezing your lower insides enough to make them pop. And it makes you literally moan like a wild animal just hit by a car. And then it stops. And then you feel fine until the next one. So, pale-faced yet with a sudden rush of excitement, we jumped into the car and drove fifteen minutes to the hospital.

I only had one more contraction on the way there and didn't have another until just before I was examined, which signalled the beginning of the transitional stage of labour for me as we soon discovered I was already eight centimetres dilated. I couldn't believe how far along I was and hadn't felt much until that previous hour.

You hear stories, don't you, of people being sent back home reeling in pain at one centimetre, and of some enduring days of slow labour before the final stage. Thankfully, I am one of the lucky ones who was completely unaware that my cervix had stretched enough to fit an apple through it before I felt a proper contraction. That meant I had much less time having to deal with working through the contractions and for that I am eternally grateful! Ladies who spend many hours and long days in labour, experiencing pains that are so hard to describe to someone who hasn't felt them yet and just never knowing when it's all going to end, I salute you. You are physically the strongest of our species, well done. Fortune would have it that my labour was over fairly quickly. Despite arriving on the ward at eight centimetres, there was enough time to fill the birthing pool, which I had so wanted to try, and get me submerged.

Now, another thing that isn't made clear to us, whilst birthing pools are great and I would indeed recommend them to anyone who has the option when they birth, once you are in there and in the midst of imminent birth, you forget to move. Either you forget, or you just can't, I'm still not sure which, but I found myself at the edge of the pool on my knees, facing outwards and leaning over the side with one hand clutching the gas and air pump, and the other squeezing my husband's hands until I had stopped his blood flow and his knuckles turned white. I was actually very comfortable except for the fact that the gas and air pump in my fist was annoying me, and after three puffs at it, I didn't feel like it was doing anything anyway, so that went, and I just held onto Ste and let Jesus take the wheel. It wasn't until a couple of days after the birth that I noticed the varnish on my toenails, which had been applied a few days before, had been scratched off by the bottom of the pool, which made me think I must have literally been curling my toes in pain when I was in there.

Thinking back to the labour, I mentioned previously that at this point in my life I was a 'mindfulness and wellbeing' type. I wholly believed (and still do to a degree) that the body follows the mind, that your thoughts become physical manifestations and that you attract back what you put out there. Hypnobirthing wasn't something I had looked into during my pregnancy. In actual fact, I hadn't even heard of it that time around, but in retrospect, I honestly think that that was what I did without realising. Gas and air moved away from me as requested, I focussed on my breathing, and thought that with every contraction, my body was opening up and allowing itself to do what every woman is built to do; bring my baby closer to the outside with every one of them.

Of course I was in pain, but I wasn't afraid, and it wasn't unbearable. The birthing pool certainly helped in that respect. I felt safe and cocooned within the soothing water. The midwife frequently checked my tummy and let me know what was happening. But then, to my absolute horror, my zen was shattered by the recognition that my pushing was not yet producing my child, but it was producing my poo. I felt that nugget pop out like a pill from a blister pack. I was mortified, but midwives are pros, and I heard the recognisable sound of a metal bin lid flipping open and closing and knew that the angel (her name was Rebecca) must have fished that sucker out of my sacred water bath and disposed of it without a hint of embarrassment. That is true nurture and care at a time when you are at your most vulnerable. At that moment, I had the ultimate respect for midwives. Their jobs go far deeper than simply delivering your baby safely. They are there at the height of your most vulnerable moment, to care, assist and nurture you through it. They witness not only joys and despair, but also the female body working in such a way that one can only describe it as a machine. They oil that machine. They keep the engine going and polish it clean for you. They are wondrously clever and passionate people who know that what you don't need when trying to evict a small human from your fanny, is to worry about it arriving in a pool of floaters. Midwives, you have my utmost respect, thank you.

The pushing continued (baby, not poo) and the sounds coming out of my mouth became primeval. Moans and groans left my mouth that my ancestors back in the beginning of time would have communicated with. Words were suddenly lost from my mind. I couldn't speak, yet literal mooing like a cow took over my vocabulary. I actually mooed! It was the only noise my throat could make with each push that expressed the physicality of what was happening. The *Mmmm* sound caught my tongue at the beginning of each contraction (which were now so close together I couldn't tell them apart) and gradually evolved into a "Mmmoooo" at the back of my throat as I pushed down. I remember the feeling of my waters breaking whilst I was submerged, like a tiny balloon popping inside me before a rush of water. Have you ever squirted when you came? It was kind of like that, except obviously not in a pleasurable way.

Three and a half hours after arriving at the hospital, and now so close to delivery, the midwives decided that I need to change position because the pushing wasn't working. Attempting to roll over and get comfortable in the reverse position, knees bent with my feet flat on the floor of the pool and elbows hooked over the side, all I could feel aside from the labour pains were pins and needles in my feet from having knelt for two hours. They hoisted me up and out of the pool, slowly and awkwardly down the steps as a head was crowning between my legs, then sat me on a little contraption that reminded me of old-fashioned milking stool crossed with a tiny toilet seat. In effect, I was squatting and by now in an upright position with Ste sat behind me holding both hands. It didn't take long for gravity to kick in and ring of fire to take hold.

Whoever coined the term 'ring of fire' knew what they were talking about. The moment when your labia and perineum (the bit of skin between your foof and your bum hole, also known as your gooch) reach maximum stretch and can expand no further without tearing, is a poignant moment during childbirth. On one hand, you know that it means the head is coming out and therefore you are so close to meeting your baby and it all being over, yet on the other hand you fear for your vagina and the fact that you actually may be about to split in half. That burning, fully expanded feeling is something I will never forget, despite them telling you that you do, "because if you didn't, nobody would go on to have more children", simply because it was extraordinary. It was in that specific moment of searing pain that I realised how empowered I felt and how truly amazing my body is. Whether I tore or not I did not care (I did have a second-degree tear, but we'll get to that in a minute), I just had this overwhelming respect for my body and what it was trying and succeeding to do. My entire pelvic region was literally disjointing and opening up to evict a seven-pound human, enabled by the hormones it had been making and pumping around it for the previous nine months. Clever stuff, eh? There was another head appearing from within that ring of skin, like a lion leaping through a blazing circus hoop. Although my baby was not leaping; she was slithering slowly like a wet snail. Let's not get into semantics though, she was on her way, nonetheless. Head poking through and ring of fire suddenly distinguished, the hardest part was over and within minutes, and with a couple of final pushes, there she was, arms and legs stretched out, looking like a purple starfish. The most beautiful purple starfish I had ever seen, with massive, alert eyes and a button nose.

Four hours after we had arrived at the hospital, she was finally here. Edging back slightly off the milk maid perch and onto the edge of the low bed, I was given an injection to make my placenta come out and waited for that happen. It felt like a bowl of jelly slipping out when it finally came, but it was swiftly removed from between my legs and then replaced by the face of a concerned looking midwife.

Having barely held Harriet, she was promptly wrapped up and given to my husband, whilst I was helped into lying position on a bed and stitched up. What I didn't know at the time, was that I was bleeding quite heavily. They gave me a further injection to help clot it and stitched me up to see if that was the issue. It wasn't. I was still bleeding. Poor Ste told me afterwards that the chair in which he sat with our brand-new baby, after just having watched me go through labour, was positioned just so that he was directly facing my now ravaged and bleeding vagina, which looked like it had just returned from a battle field. He witnessed the overflow and the stitches at an angle which I imagine would now enable him to produce a lovely cross stitch embroidery from memory. But it wasn't over yet. As three more midwives (one of them was possibly a doctor, but I can't remember) entered the room and observed the wreckage, my main midwife declared that I was still bleeding and because I couldn't force myself to wee, I needed a catheter fitting, but in order to do that they were going to have to tear a couple of the stitches they had just put in. Honestly, for the first time since feeling that contraction at home on the landing, I felt scared of the pain I might be about to feel. And holy shit – I was right. As the catheter was fitted, the scream that left my mouth was louder and more distressed than any of the sounds I had made during labour. I suddenly disliked my midwife and very much wanted to clamp my thighs shut on her face between them which such a force that she would be crushed. Of my entire labour experience, whatever happened to me in that moment (again, I'm still not 100% certain as I couldn't see) that was the worst bit. It must have worked though because I remember peeing onto my freshly torn, stitched, then torn again, noony and yelping in pain from the burning sensation. They administered another injection into my leg and told me that if this one didn't halt the bleeding, then I would have to be taken to the labour ward from the birthing centre suite. Thank goodness, within a few minutes the bleeding had eventually slowed down enough that they could tidy up stitches and they were happy I was alright. Labour number one done.

Although I was expecting to feel sore and tired immediately after the birth, I wasn't expecting the feeling of breathlessness that I had. I remember standing up and trying to walk across the room to the toilet, but literally not being able to stand up straight because my diaphragm felt like it had gone limp. The midwives assured me it was normal and that I just had to take it easy on my feet until I felt like I could straighten up enough to breathe properly. It makes sense really. I had just used muscles in my body that I didn't know existed to push out and expel a 7lb 3oz human from it. In hindsight, perhaps that is another reason why the breathing techniques they teach you are so important. I literally couldn't catch my breath. I felt like I had been punched in the abs and winded.

We had made the choice prior to the arrival that we wanted to formula feed so that we could share the experience, which was good given that I was unable to breast feed straight after birth due to my heavy bleeding and Harriet being given straight to Ste for first skin to skin. I know for many that these first hours can be daunting as they see whether a baby will latch and attempt to feed, and although the midwives with us were great and never actually said it, I did still feel an unspoken pressure to try the breast rather than formula. But we stuck to our guns and were showed how to feed and wind.

As it was a quiet shift in the birthing centre and our first baby, they allowed us to stay in our suite until we felt ready to go home and we were so grateful. Like all new parents, we were utterly clueless what to do with this tiny human. They pulled a double bed down from a hidden compartment in the wall and placed Harriet next to us in a plastic cot, then left us for a couple of hours to bond and rest in our little bubble. I think we ended up staying there for most of the day before feeling ready to make a move late afternoon, when we had the next challenge of mastering the bloody car seat.

It was pissing down with rain outside as we faffed and tutted trying to figure out what strap went where and how it attached to the car seat belt safely, all the while trying to shelter our brand-new baby from the elements as though a drop of rain hitting her might trigger the plague. Home time and chippy tea brought the whole incredible experience to an end and the next chapter of our lives to a beginning.

Going into labour with Ted was a different story. After being informed at my acupuncture induction around 4 p.m. that I was already four to five centimetres dilated, I was prepared for the inevitable that evening. Grandparents were called to pick Harriet up from nursery and a bag of her things delivered to them, uncertain how long she would be there but hopeful that we would all be back home as a family of four the following night. The house was quiet for a few hours before Ste returned home from work with just me and the dog enjoying a rare few hours of peace and quiet.

By 9 p.m., I still wasn't feeling anything, so we went to bed to try and cram in a few hours sleep, knowing what was in store for us very soon. I woke at 11 p.m. with mild cramps and sprung into action (as much as a heavily pregnant woman can spring). Terrified after my short four-hour labour with Harriet that this one was going to appear even more quickly, I rang Amy, my midwife, who appeared at my house within half an hour. Still only experiencing very mild cramping, she examined me on the couch and said that I was already about eight centimetres. Shit the bed! I didn't want a home birth. All I could think was: a) go me, no major contractions and I'd made it this far, and b) get me to that hospital NOW. She followed our car in hers and we arrived at the hospital to park in exactly the same spot we had parked in when we had Harriet.

She led us onto the birthing centre to exactly the same room I had given birth to Harriet in. Labour took exactly the same amount of time it took to deliver Harriet and they were almost exactly the same weight. Déjà vu. It was fate.

Arriving on the ward, Amy had already called ahead, and the pool was ready and waiting for me. Only as we began to prepare ourselves, chatting casually and picking on snacks from the hospital bag we had packed, it occurred to me that we were so chilled out and relaxed about it all that the little cramps I'd been having had stopped. After a while, Amy examined me and said that given how calm I was we could end up being there a while before things kicked off again, so she asked if I wanted her to break my waters to get things moving again. Yes, I did. I wanted anything to get that baby out.

Unlike my previous experience of waters breaking during labour whilst I was submerged in the pool, I felt this one more. When they broke, there was a distinctive popping sound followed by a flood of warm liquid that gushed onto my thighs and seeped around my lower back. It had been a long time since I'd wet myself to such capacity, but I imagine it's a similar feeling to wetting yourself in bed. Job done, the contractions started again within the hour and this time they were not little cramps. These were full-blown rushes of adrenaline and tension, only this time I recognised it and knew how to deal with them mentally, thanks to some research into hypnobirthing and breathing techniques.

For anyone reading this and considering hypnobirthing as an option – do it. It isn't as hippy-dippy as it sounds. It basically teaches you to control your pain and anxiety by understanding the physical phases your body is going through to get the baby out and helps you to stay calm and focussed on the positive aspect that with every contraction, that tiny human is closer to being in your arms and no longer inside you. It's an amazing way of harnessing your thoughts and using them to trust your body, easing any fears and doubts as you experience them. Add to this the birthing pool and it's just a winning combination that I highly recommend if you are low risk and able to do so.

Gas and air was my friend the second time around. I was in the same position in the birthing pool as I was the first time around, kneeling down with my knees facing outwards, and I chugged on that gas as I felt the grip of each stomach-churning spasm, although I was still able to remain calm and focus on my breathing.

The drug had a peculiar effect on me. At one point I declared that I felt like an octopus. Great hallucinogenic. Just as they had done so the last time, the moos and moans echoed from the back of my throat, except I felt totally in control of when I voiced them, plus I might add that I did not shit myself second time around. Yay! (Although I genuinely don't think I would have cared if I had this time.)

I was definitely in a confident and strong state of mind this time, so when the ring of fire started to flare up, I was ready for it. Panting quickly (something I learnt on YouTube, which apparently can reduce tearing as well as keep you focussed), I felt like I was conquering the world in that moment.

Once again, my wonderful warrior body was proving why women are such absolute queens. I could do this. I had done it before when I was less prepared, and this time I was so ready. I breathed a huge sigh of relief after delivering the head, mistakenly thinking that it was all done and he was here, until Amy said, "Now the shoulders next and the rest of him." Bugger. I thought I'd gotten off lightly. But the next contraction saw him swiftly evicted from my vagina and into the warm water pool, where he was scooped up into my arms, cord still attached to the placenta still inside of me and wrapped in a towel. Hello, Teddy Arthur!

We sat there breathing in his gorgeous purple chubbiness, his little chicken legs, his perfect lips and his tiny winky. He was perfect.

Another note on the birthing pool at this point — nobody tells you that once you've delivered you're literally sitting in a blood bath. As I held my new little man with my husband instinctively beside us (on the outside of the pool obviously), I couldn't help but notice that my war wound was leaking into the pool, turning it redder and redder by the minute. It looked like a shark attack had just taken place and I was the victim. I asked Amy if that was normal and she said yes, they had ways of monitoring blood loss and what was a safe level, so that reassured me somewhat. Although, I have to admit, I did not enjoy sitting in a pool of my own blood and clots until my placenta delivered itself about half an hour later. I was also freezing by that point and very much ready to get out.

Although I'd gained another second-degree tear and needed a few stitches, there were no risky incidents like after delivering Harriet, and after another four hour labour, the whole thing had been textbook perfect. Three had become four.

Just as we had planned the first time around, we decided to formula and bottle-feed Ted. But in the moments after giving birth, as I sat in the birthing water with my new man nuzzled into my breast, I was overcome by the urge to give breast feeding a try. I mentioned it to Amy and she showed me how to hold him and position his head to help him find my nipple as we waited with baited breath to see if he latched on.

My nipples have always been on the small side – bee stings at the best of times – so I was rather chuffed when his tiny mouth found it and went for gold. Having never researched it or considered breast feeding, pride was momentarily replaced by shock at the painful pinching feeling of his hard little gums as my boob became breakfast. It hurt. I didn't complain though, as I assumed it was normal and obviously thousands of women do this for months, don't they? So, I said nothing and winced through the experience waiting for him to stop. In the next twenty-four hours that followed, I breast fed him a few more times from alternating nipples, experiencing the same pain and eventually admitting it to a ward midwife when my nipples began to bleed. She suggested a couple of other ways to hold him and things to help relieve it, but the pain didn't stop until we arrived home with him and I instructed Ste to plug in the perfect prep machine and get the formula tub out. I quit. I'd tried and I'd done a day, but I didn't want to continue. And do you know what? That's okay, I didn't feel guilty. I wasn't weak. The little guy was still getting fed and nourished. I'd given it my best shot, but on top of all the other aches and pains that giving birth brings, I didn't want to add bleeding, scabby nipples and a hungry baby to the equation. Breast feeding is not for the faint hearted; you've got to be strong to handle that shit and I hold my hands up, it wasn't for me. To those who try it and succeed, I salute you and your nipples of steel.

Another aspect immediately following the birth that I was better prepared for this time around, was the first pee. I was ready for it this time, just praying no catheter or intervention would be needed. I was lucky and it wasn't, so when I felt the call of tinkle I marched (like John Wayne) across the floor from bed to bathroom armed with my water bottle with a squeezy spout. Ladies, it helps. Always go into labour with an empty squeezable water bottle nearby and use it to relive the pain of first urination by squeezing cold water onto your vaj when you pee. I did this for every wee for at least 24 hours. The first number two is another story, but we will discuss that in chapter three.

Just as after my first labour, we were afforded the luxury of staying in our private birthing suite in the birthing centre after Ted was born. Although we felt more like we knew what we were doing this time around, we were grateful to be able to move at our own pace and enjoy the tranquillity of our little newborn bubble on our own instead of a busy ward.

Ted had arrived at 04:10, and by 11:00, we had our bags packed and car seat ready, waiting to be discharged and get back to our home comforts. The midwives just had to do a few more last-minute routine checks on Ted, which is when it all went a bit tits up.

Despite appearing completely healthy and breathing fine on his own, his oxygen levels were low. We became nervous as a doctor was called and more and more professionals gathered around him on the little table. After two hours of monitoring, they determined that he was okay, but his levels were low enough to cause concern, so they wanted us to stay put for the day to keep an eye on him and monitor him hourly. Thank goodness he gradually improved, and his levels rose to a normal number by that evening, meaning that we were discharged around 10 p.m. and allowed to go home. It was scary and we couldn't help but worry, but midwives are miraculous creatures, and we were in very good hands. We were all well looked after and still they let us stay on in the birthing suite rather than move us to the labour or neo-natal wards. So off we went, with a stop at McDonalds drive through for tea, before heading home to settle into the new 'normal'.

Harriet returned home the following morning to a new baby brother; a priceless moment we managed to catch on video and one which will stay with me forever. My heart was so full of love, it felt fit to burst.

So, Mama, you've had a baby. You have pushed your body to the edge of its pain threshold and made noises from within you that would frighten wild animals. You may have been overcome by nausea, you may have feared for a life, you may have been cut by metal, you may have shit yourself in front of a stranger and you may have torn your gooch to shreds, but regardless of whether your baby arrived via the boot or the sunroof, you have created and delivered a life into this world. Your child. And I hope that whatever the circumstances you went through to do that, you recognised just how much of a warrior you are. Respect to your body for enabling it to happen. Respect to your mind for getting you through it. Respect to the health professionals who guided you and kept you safe. Women, love your bodies. Look at what they can do.

And despite the pain, the unknown, the physical torment of it all, I can honestly say hand on heart that I really enjoyed both of my labours.

Experiencing it the first time was the thing that made me want another child. I just found the whole thing so incredibly empowering and inspiring. Sure, it hurt and yes, if you'd ask in the moment if I was enjoying it, I'd have punched you, yet nothing can describe the feeling of bringing a child into the world. It's like an out-of-body experience that ends with you waking up as a different person. You can't not change. You can't undo it. So, you accept that you did do it with pride and knowledge.

Yes, I enjoyed my labours and births, but I will not be doing it for a third time. Not because of the pain, but because of what became of life immediately afterwards.

3.

Postpartum recovery

Leaking from every orifice

After every war and battle comes the recovery and reconstruction. The same can be said for childbirth. The weeks and months that follow are a time for healing, re-adjusting, a fresh perspective and rebuilding.

Let's begin with the obvious wounds, starting with the vagina and surrounding areas. Upon arriving home with my first child, I was very aware of the stitches that were keeping my battered perineum held together: a) because I couldn't sit down and b) because I was absolutely dreading going to the toilet.

Twenty-four hours into our new life as parents, we had a routine visit from a stern looking midwife who was there to do all the usual checks on Harriet. After she had carried out her duties, she asked me how I was feeling and whether I had any questions. Anxious to know that everything was okay down there, I asked her if she would have a quick look at my stitches even though I didn't have any symptoms that suggested otherwise. It's also true that once you give birth you generally do not have any qualms about getting your bits out in front of people. She informed me everything was looking good, before turning to pack her belongings up and farting loudly. Mortified, she hurried out of the house and we never saw that midwife again. Oh, if only I'd have told her in that moment that just 48 hours ago one of her team had been fishing my shit out of water for me, maybe she wouldn't have felt so embarrassed.

About a year after having my second baby, I began to experience an itch around my clitoris which provided no other symptoms than the feeling I had rubbed my prize jewel on nettles. After attempting the obvious DIY remedies (non-fragranced washing powder and switching to fragrance free vag wash instead of treating my bits to a shower in a jasmine blossom infused rainforest), it continued to the point that I was afraid to let myself or my husband flick it.

A quick trip to the gynae consultant left me with new information.

Apparently, I had torn my clitoral hood during labour and what I was experiencing was the result of scar tissue. Why it took a year to disclose itself, I do not know, but I was given a hormonal wonder cream that I was informed was the female equivalent of Viagra and would have me urging to shag like a dog on heat within three months. Said cream was the only way I could forgive my kids for the irreparable damage they had inflicted on my mangled wizard's sleeve. But yeah, clitoral hood tear. Who knew? I certainly never considered it given that both of my babies were born average sizes and weights with lovely labours, albeit rather quickly.

Scary poo, unpredictable wind and a cavernous hole

After having both kids, I found the prospect of the first poo incredibly daunting. I was expecting it to feel like a second birth, only through my anus; the one area down there that was still relatively in-tact. I wasn't wrong. I had been pre-warned by my sister who had told me to use one of my maternity pads to press firmly on the gooch close to the stitches but not on them as I felt the need to push out the poo. Now I'm not going to lie, this method did have a positive effect and it definitely did help me to feel like I was somewhat in control of the situation, but the fear of getting the giant poo that was emerging from within on my fingers as I held the pad in place proper sent me under. Five minutes later, the job was done and I felt so much better. That said, the fact it had been a few days since my last poo, and the fact that my insides had been through so much, meant that an oversized, hard monster poo was inevitable. I've never had anal sex and still to this day take great pride in the fact that my arsehole is probably the only remaining tight orifice left in my body, so the prospect of tearing it with post-birth constipation was not one I welcomed.

I learnt from this a valuable lesson which I took with me to my second birth – stool softeners. I packed a pack in my hospital bag the second time around and started popping those bad boys as soon as I could stand up, which did seem to do the trick when it came to post-birth poo after having Ted, along with the maternity pad trick.

Having spoken to a friend who endured a last-minute c-section, she informed me that it is quite common for mothers to have to manually remove the first poo themselves due to a mixture of the results of drugs, a lack of pressure to push down there after major abdominal surgery, and general fear.

Remaining on the subject of poo, let's look realistically into the future of your bowel movements once you have given birth. You might think it an obvious change that your periods are notably different, but I'll bet nobody ever told you about Period Poos?

Prior to having a baby, we women understand that there is something about our time of the month that can cause us mild disruption to the usual digestion and expulsion process, be it more frequent, less frequent, changes in colour, etc. However, once you've supported a growing baby in your lower body and pelvic region, something happens to your bowels that causes them to protest in great irritation at the monthly announcement of Aunt Flow – trapped wind. It feels a lot like you need to go, and your colon is twisting itself causing air bubbles as though it is trying to take some kind of savage revenge on you for squashing it with a growing foetus for nine months. Once you do go, it's like a rapid release of air and excrement. Literally a shit show; a dirty protest. Farts slip out and surprise you when you least expect them. Your entire nether region decides to take matter into its own hands, so that you can't predict whether the gas inside your body is going to make you seize up in pain or embarrassment.

Whilst we are on the topic of unpredictable air, let's give a round of applause to fanny-farts, shall we? Those beauties just love to announce themselves uninvited right at the crucial moment of sexy time when your partner whips you over onto your knees for a bit of doggy with a loud and wet *I am massive now! Hear me roar*! The timing is always the same and always enough to make you laugh into the pillow, but rest assured, mean don't care. They actually get a thrill out of how wet you must be down there to make that sound.

Also, along the topic of your now unrecognisably stretched vagina, I'd like to enlighten you to the fact that it gets thirsty when you put it near water, like a Gremlin. You'll go to take a long, relaxing, hot bubble bath, dry yourself off afterwards, apply your skin tonics, put on fresh clean pyjamas, then about quarter of an hour later, like a dam breaking without warning, your cervix releases a flood of reserved bath water to rival the Thames into your clean, dry undies.

We went to Center Parcs as a family recently with some close friends, and as we mums do, the two of us managed to disappear for an afternoon in the spa. A jacuzzi, a heated outdoor pool, and a hydrotherapy area were totally on our hitlist as we spent an hour or so relaxing whilst waiting to be called for our pre-booked facials and massages. For those of you who have experienced Center Parcs, you'll appreciate the glory of the enormous, fluffy waffle robes they give you to use to cover yourself when getting around the spa – they really do signify comfort and relaxation. What they also do is hide the unpreventable and unpredictable gush of half a swimming pool as you walk across the spa to your treatment room when called in. All I could do, as I sat on the leather chair filling in my health forms with my waffle robe wrapped around me, was pray that by attempting a few pelvic floor exercises, I could close off the tap before I had to lie down on the massage bed. When the therapist came for me, I slowly stood up and felt the towelling robe stick to my arse with an oddly comforting sensation of warm water – similar to how I imagine a baby must feel in their nappy. Yes ladies, it will happen to you. Not necessarily in public, but your fanny will get thirsty, so be prepared for that. Your pelvic floor will never be the same again. I can't stress enough how important it is to do your Kegel exercises during pregnancy and generally ALL THE TIME. You will be very lucky if you can join in with star-jumps and not piss on the exercise mat during your cardio class after giving birth vaginally, and you will be unlikely to ever be able to enjoy a trampoline ever again, but just to clarify, you do not piss yourself after having a bath or a swim; it is literally just the water you've been submerged in.

Adult nappies (AKA maternity pads)

Moving onwards, let me address maternity pads. Now obviously, you expect to be losing a substantial amount of blood from the battle site for a while after giving birth vaginally. Having never really experienced heavy periods (something that has massively changed over the years following birth), I found this quite weird. The blood has a smell to it. It's not bad (that would mean infection), but it's like an earthy, sweet smell which I thought of as a reminder that my insides were working hard to repair themselves. This iron-rich odour tends to accompany all future periods to a certain degree after having children. Mine definitely have a much more distinct smell to them now; not unpleasant but distinct.

Maternity pads are huge and uncomfortable, but a crucial element of your immediate post-birth recovery kit. Normal sanitary pads would be too thin, and the perforated fabric they are made from poses a risk to any exposed stitches. Therefore, your only option really is these enormous pads. Or so I thought, until the second time around when I discovered the joy of adult nappy pants, created specifically for incontinence. I might have been matching my baby's disposable nappied appearance, but those stretchy, soft, supportive padded undies gave me life. I didn't need to ruin any knickers and they made the blood loss in the first few days so much more bearable. After a couple of weeks, when the bleeding was slowing down, I found that the local supermarket sold slimline maternity pads, similar to regular sanitary pads but made from a softer, more absorbent material. Moving on to using these felt like another step forward in recovery for me, although it was six months before I braved going back to tampons. I think it took about four months before I got my first period, but I continued to use pads for at least another two months after that when I also realised that my bucket fadge now required super plus sized tampons to avoid any leakage. Honestly, it's like throwing a hotdog down the M6.

Booby fountains

The topic of leaking leads me nicely to breast milk. I had started to leak colostrum about a month before I was due in both pregnancies, so I had stocked up on breast pads. When I was pregnant with Harriet, despite leaning towards formula feeding, I also treated myself to a few pretty nursing bras so I could avoid any underwiring and have the option to breast feed if I changed my mind. I quickly learnt that my gym bras were a far better idea once breast feeding was not happening, because the pads stayed in place better and I had more support. There's something empowering about the first night you get to sleep without a bra on when your milk dries up too. It's heaven.

My milk came in about three days after both of my births, accompanied by shooting pains and very hard, sensitive boobs. Having always been fairly flat chested, milk boobs were an absolutely joy. Hands down, it was one of my favourite parts of pregnancy. I went from wearing a 34A (as I had been for many years) to a 34C and I spent at least five minutes every morning marvelling at my new girls in the mirror. To my dismay, they only lasted until my breast milk dried up. However, I have been left with a comfortable B cup after two children, so all is not totally lost. Plus, after speaking to women I know who did breast feed, I have been informed that I should consider myself lucky that my little speed bumps are still rather pert and my nipples sit right where they belong. As someone who lusted for a breast enhancement for many years, I have now learnt to love my trusty little tits, but it took becoming a mother to arrive at that place.

When one of my best friends (who didn't have children by that point) arrived at our house for a visit after I had just had Harriet, I asked her to bring a Savoy cabbage round. Confused, but not wanting to question the requests of a hormonal, sleep deprived new mum, she came bearing the gift, which I promptly stashed to chill in the fridge before putting a leaf in each bra cup, between the boob and the breast pad. Ladies, it sounds mental, but it really does work if you're trying to dry your milk up. The cold leaves help to soothe as well as containing some kind of chemical which helps to draw the milk out. I did this for about a week and I wholly believe it sped up the process. I have heard it can help soothe mastitis too, as long as you don't overdo it. My boobs leaked for around 5 weeks after each baby before completely stopping, but everybody is different. Bearing in mind that I only breast fed for 24 hours after my second, I never really got past the colostrum phase, and I don't recall my hormones being massively effected during the process, I don't think that was bad going.

Mum-Tums

In the days and weeks following the arrival of bubs, I was amazed at the way my body shape changed as it began the healing process.

So, once you've given birth (whichever way it happens) your organs and insides are still all over the place for a while from whichever temporary location they were pushed and rearranged into to make room for your growing baby. Before conceiving my first, I was a healthy UK size eight. I fucking hate exercise, but at that time I had been making a conscious effort to visit the gym at least once or twice a week, so I was fairly toned and happy with the way I looked. Watching my bump grow throughout each trimester until it was heavy and very hard was both fascinating and encouraging, but I knew there would be changes I'd have to face; stretch marks, saggy skin, possible scarring etc., all of which I spent the whole nine months mentally preparing for. It worked, because instead of feeling anxious about what my body was going to look like once I became a mother, I totally embraced it. I rubbed oil on my belly and thighs every day but took no other precautions except telling myself that my body was incredible. What it was doing was incredible. The ways in which it was altering itself to accommodate pregnancy was incredible, and whatever I would be left with afterwards would be the physical manifestation of all that incredible.

Throughout my first pregnancy I documented the progress. I stood sideways and frontways in front of our long bedroom mirror and took photos on the first weekend of every month, in the same tie-top bikini, then continued this process for about four months after the birth. Not because I was obsessed with regaining my pre-baby shape, but purely because I was in awe of myself and wanted a record of the journey. That said, I did make the decision to try a vegan diet at 17 weeks post-partum with the goal to shift some of the remaining weight for a wedding I was attending that summer, so I obviously felt some degree of pressure to look a certain way. My jelly belly mum-tum gradually reduced week by week until I was left with a little pouch of skin, enough to hang over the top of my waistband and restrict me from comfortably wearing tight belts, yet a good enough handful for an excellent excuse to go shopping for new high-rise jeans and trousers. I call it my baby bum bag. It's the part of my body that gives me the most pride whilst simultaneously giving me the most annoyance.

Now, you will have noticed by this point that I'm all about promoting positive body image and preaching 'love your skin', but even I have fallen victim to society's unrealistic and unhealthy judgement of body shapes and sizes. Bodycon dresses have become a big no for me. Crop tops have also gone, along with bikinis in favour of a flattering all-in-one swimsuit. I'm just far too self-conscious that my abs aren't flat anymore, and I annoy myself with it.

Four years in, and I'm still learning to adjust to my new shape, despite being mostly at peace with it. Let's face it, I'm no spring chicken anymore either, and I like my food and a drink, so after two kids it would be weird if I did still look the same.

All the above points have helped me appreciate my shape for what it is.

I have curvy hips where I never used to – widened from birthing; I have boobs bigger than previously – enlarged from the ability to feed my children had I chosen to; I have a belly where it used to be flat – the home that kept my babies safe for nine months; I have thread veins in my legs which were once flawless – an area that held my body up despite a massive weight gain.

Cramps from hell and PMT

Post-partum cramping was a big issue for me after my second child – another glorious side-effect to healing that nobody had told me about that I wasn't expecting. It makes sense that after giving birth, your uterus needs time to revert back to the size it was before housing a baby. In the days immediately after giving birth, after-pains are common as the uterus contracts in a bid to shrink back. I didn't experience any sensation of this after having Harriet, or if I did, I was too sleep-deprived and running on adrenaline to notice them. But after having Ted, my lower abdomen felt like it was trying to squeeze itself down through my pelvis the same way the baby had come. It was agony, but all I could do was rotate paracetamol and ibuprofen and ride it out. Apparently, so I am told, pelvic cramping (or 'afterbirth' pains) is very common and usually gets worse with each child you bear. I'm not sure how true that is or if the science behind it if it is correct, but I shall not be having a third child to find out. If you've experienced this and it has gotten worse each time, I commend you because it fucking wrecks. Having never really experienced period pains, light cramping before my period has become a slightly unappealing, lasting after-effect since giving birth, but it isn't something debilitating enough for me to worry about. A couple of paracetamols usually hits the spot and relieves it.

The same cannot be said for my PMT though. I have become a raging, fire-breathing, psycho bitch for an average three days of the month. The only major PMT symptom I had before kids was a hormone headache a few days before coming on which actually stopped when I came off birth control. Yet, these days I can time the arrival of my period almost to the hour purely by the unjustifiable and uncontrollable emotional mood swings I experience like clockwork three days beforehand. Now, I can't blame this entirely on having carried two children as it could just be age related, but it is coincidental that this ailment began immediately after having children, when my hormone balance shifted. It could just be that the children themselves cause me to lose my shit easily and relentlessly, but I am definitely more irritable and less patient in the lead up to menstruating. I snap quickly and I ugly cry more often as well as getting the red mist and shouting a lot at anyone who displeases me. For three days, I am usually extremely out of character and more of a twat than usual, then as soon as I come on, I resume normal female twattishness at an acceptable level.

Not everybody gets the immediate 'love rush

One final yet vital point I wish to bring to light about the realities of the first hours of motherhood, and one which I find gets thrown about a lot rather insensitively and rather ignorantly, is that 'feeling you get when your baby is placed into your arms'. Let's take a moment to think about this shall we?

How many of you were told about the magical qualities of this life defining moment? How many of you were assured that "once that baby appears, you forget all about the trauma down there"? Which of us were fully expecting to look deep into our newborn's eyes and feel a rush of love like we would never be able to put into words? These are common statements in my experience, usually made idly to most mothers-to-be by Doris, the 80-year-old neighbour or Harmony, the 20-year-old eco-junkie who runs the local breastfeeding clinic despite having never been pregnant or given birth herself. These comments are always made with the best intention and as a reassurance to an expecting mother. But Doris and Harmony need to know that they aren't always correct, and in offering their well wishes and words of wisdom, they might potentially be doing more harm than good.

You see, I longed for my babies. I was excited to meet both of them and welcome them into the world, yet admittedly it took me around four months to feel that unconditional bond with my first child (and that was without a hint of PND) and an even longer eight months with my second (although granted, my mental health was not good at that time).

After giving birth to both of my children, I can honestly say that I never felt that immediate rush of overwhelming love that I expected to feel, despite having heard it said so many times beforehand. Of course, I loved them and was thrilled to have them arrive all healthy and cute, but I just never got 'that feeling'. I'm not alone in saying this. I have admitted it to other mothers who agree with me, that although the love was there, it took a while to feel the bond. Maybe it was because the first few weeks are usually spent in some kind of shock and adjustment period It seems fair to me to assume that the bond can come once the dust starts to settle and new mums begin to find their feet a bit. There is no evidence to suggest that breastfeeding stimulates a bond stronger than formula fed babies, either. Both methods provide an opportunity to gaze into each other's eyes and reflect on the journey together so far. So, can we please stop inciting this notion that mothers are expected to feel an instant bond to their new babies from the moment they exit the womb? Because, in reality, it doesn't always work like that. It doesn't make you any less of a doting and loving parent. It doesn't necessarily mean that you have a mental health issue or that you are incapable of growing the bond with your child. Just give it some time.

You've just been through massive trauma, albeit a joyful one, so go easy on yourself. As long as you accept that your first priority has just evolved into your new child, and as long as you feel the pride and love in the room, as long as that baby and you are healthy, don't panic that you don't feel 'the feeling' straight away. It will come, I promise, and when it does, it's the most breath taking, reality-kick ever. A bond between you and another human that you brought into this world which can never be broken.

4.

Postnatal Depression

The unwelcome house guest

As I sit here with my now clear mind, reflecting upon what to write here, it feels like I could write an entire book based solely on this chapter, but deep down I know that my own personal experience of this mother-fucker will be very different from so many others. Like pregnancy and labour, it is such a personal thing, and no two experiences are likely to be the same. But for the sake of trying to get women to open up about it and improve awareness and honesty around the subject, I'm going to attempt to explain this hell from my perspective in an unfiltered and savagely honest way – once I figure out where to start. It's so hard trying to explain what is going on in your head when you don't even know yourself. I should probably note at this point, that I really tried to keep this chapter light and wanted to inject some humour into my words. However, upon spewing out my thoughts, I found it so hard to think of ways to do that. So it is raw and maybe a little more subdued than the rest of the book, but maybe that is necessary, given the severity of the subject matter. I even asked close friends if they could recall any funny anecdotes or words which we exchanged during this time that would lighten the load, but even they couldn't think of a time when we smiled about it. Bear with me; I promise I will get back to being a clown afterwards.

Antenatal Depression

Finding out I was pregnant with Ted came as a slight shock but not a total earthquake. We were at that early stage of trying where you're not *trying* but not *not trying,* so getting that positive test result after only six weeks was happy news albeit sooner than we expected. From the beginning, I felt noticeably different to how I'd felt the first time around. There was no impulse buying of tiny clothes that we did not need. There was no time spent idly daydreaming about the future or what baby might look like. There was no scrolling the internet for nursery ideas or feeling overly protective of my belly and needing to stroke it at all times. Maternity clothes were not bought until I could physically no longer fit in my usual clothes, and although I didn't partake in alcohol or drugs, I certainly did not look after myself the same way I did when I was pregnant with Harriet. Everything was off. The lack of excitement or attachment made me feel shit, so I would push it to the back of my mind and tell myself that I was just busy parenting a toddler and balancing life and that it was normal to feel different second time around, since I had already 'been there and done it once.' I never admitted it to a single soul. Not my husband, not my midwife, not my friends. Nobody knew that although I was happy to be pregnant, I just wasn't *feeling it* – or myself. All the warning signs for antenatal depression were there, yet not once did it occur to me, *#blessedhelen*, that I was firmly in that scary camp. Truth be told, I did not even know at that time that such an illness existed. At routine midwife appointments, I would use my usual sarcasm and humour to veil the reality of my responses to their questions, hiding behind the façade of 'just a regular pregnant mum with a toddler at home' to dodge the reality that I was not okay. I don't recall during that pregnancy ever being asked if I was excited or prepared. Maybe that was why I never told the truth, because the moment never presented itself to come clean. I wasn't unhappy or anxious. I didn't feel sad or angry or any obvious negative emotion. I just wasn't that arsed about it. Pregnancy was not my thing. I did not enjoy it, so I wonder whether it was me repeatedly telling myself this that played a part in my emotional unravelling. You attract back what you put out there, right?

For nine months, I felt like I was just going through the motions: take care of myself, eat well, go to appointments, avoid stress (easier said than done when you already have one Tiny biting at your ankles), buy in the essentials, choose a name, look after that precious little bean inside of you, etc. On the surface, I looked and behaved like any other grateful, pregnant mother, yet inside I was already becoming numb. Deep down, I knew that my overly-nonchalant feelings of being pregnant with my planned-for baby were not normal.

Upon his arrival, I was genuinely chuffed to bits with the belter I had grown, and we had produced. He was beautiful. Holding him in my arms and talking to him about meeting his big sister whilst my proud husband beamed at me, I displayed all the usual behaviours of a new mother and I genuinely felt like myself for the first time in months, but it was short lived. The blissful, newborn bubble feeling of euphoria lasted only a few days before the nasty emptiness began to creep back in, and I desperately attempted to convince myself that I was fine, just tired. Again, I mentioned it to nobody, so sure that either: a) it was normal for the second time around and it would go away, b) if I did in fact raise the conversation of how I really felt, people would make a fuss, or c) I was imagining the whole thing and I was really fine. It was so confusing.

Symptoms

At around eight weeks old, Ted started to change in a worrying way. He seemed uncomfortable and began to bring every feed back up. He became cranky and inconsolable. Gone was the chilled sleeping baby of those first days. He was 'waking up' like a fucking angry, erupting volcano. We wouldn't get his severe reflux diagnosis for another ten months after that, after a lot of painfully long and loud sleepless nights and massive anxiety about what was wrong with him and what we could do to end his discomfort. But I do believe that this was the tipping point for my fragile mind. The time where everything began to spiral.

It was Christmas before the subject of my mental health was brought up by anyone. That *someone* being my wonderful mother-in-law. Ted was about four-month-old, and I was seriously struggling. Unable to hide behind humour and a smile any longer, I was obviously not myself and had gotten to the point where I couldn't be arsed trying to hide it anymore. My thoughts were muddled (if I could think at all). It was as though there was a cloud inside my brain and just stringing a sentence together was difficult. My mind was a mash-up of nonsensical thoughts, and I couldn't organise them or make sense of them at all. They were not exactly intrusive thoughts (I was not suicidal, and I wasn't worried about any harm coming to my children), they were more like confused musings or relentless questions to myself about where the fuck my head had gone. Somebody asked me to describe what was going on in my head and I used this metaphor; do you remember seeing the scene immediately after the 9/11 terror attacks when the towers had collapsed? There were hundreds of sheets of paper slowly drifting down through the dust-filled skies like feathers, eventually settling onto the chalky, unswept, rubble-covered pavements. That was how I visualised my mind. My thoughts were like those pieces of paper; a myriad of irrelevant tasks and musings which collectively floated around every corner of my brain, every moment of every day without pause, disturbing the dusty layer that my brain felt lined with. Yet, I couldn't verbalise any of those thoughts, because my concentration levels were so low that they wouldn't allow me to organise them. I knew what I wanted to do, and I knew what I needed to do, but it was as though there was a physical barrier preventing me from doing it.

I recall one Thursday afternoon sitting at my laptop desperately attempting to work and catch up on some time I had missed. I had the brief in my head and my notes in front of me, but I couldn't stop myself from breaking down on my husband because I literally could not for the life of me devise a simple sentence and transform it from my thoughts to my fingertips to type.

My body physically ached from head to toe, and every so often I would feel totally void of any feelings whatsoever. Just numb. I was on autopilot as far as looking after my family was concerned, once again just going through the motions and completing the daily tasks that were necessary to keep everyone else healthy and happy. The sleep deprivation was far more intense than I remembered the first time around which had also taken its toll alongside the fact that we hadn't had much, if any, help with nor breaks from the baby. I was a mess, a shell of a person; there was nothing left inside of me except blood and bones.

My personal hygiene began to suffer, not in a 'new mum doesn't have time to shower way', yet not as drastic as a teenage boy way. Some days, I would forget to brush my teeth. It would get to bedtime before I'd realised. On other days, I would shove on the same clothes as the previous two days because I knew I wasn't going to see anybody and just about remember to spray deodorant. There were days when I'd stand in the shower, knowing I really should wash my hair, but deciding that dry shampoo and a bobble could get me through another day because I didn't even the energy to lift the hair dryer afterwards. Washing my face consisted of using a baby wipe to get the sleep out of my eyes. My daily uniform became a range of hoodies and jeans. They were easy to shove on, comfortable to parent in, warm and practical, yet not a thought for style or the way I used to dress which made me feel confident and celebrated my individuality. Gradually, the waistbands on my jeans and the shoulders on my tops became baggy and loose as I lost too much weight. Even my knicker elastic was failing me and falling around my hips. Food was not a priority. I wasn't starving myself, but I only ate when I fancied it and would casually pick at biscuits and fruit throughout the day with a proper evening meal because I'd cooked it for the family, so I might as well partake. Having previously been a massive foodie, it was another passion lost to the battle and another one of my character traits surrendered, which in hindsight obviously contributed to my fatigue and low energy.

The most noticeable and potentially the most disturbing symptom I repeatedly experienced was the rage. This was the first symptom I personally recognised as being a problem. It would sneak up on me out of nowhere in a moment of stress or anxiety and I would absolutely blow, instantly changing from being someone who promoted calm and positivity. It absolutely blind-sided me as I would feel my heart start to beat faster and feel the unavoidable lump in my throat before uncontrollably screeching like a dying cat at my kids, full on dragon mode. A red mist would come over my head in which I couldn't think rationally and had zero self-control over. Shouting was the only way I could verbalise what I need to in those seconds, yet I knew that with every awful yell, I could be damaging the harmonious home I wanted my children to feel secure in. I felt like a monster. And then the cycle of guilt would start again. What kind of mother was I? They were just babies. How could I speak to them in that way? They didn't understand. I was supposed to be the rational adult teaching them. Harriet would be so confused having had the mother she'd had for two years suddenly turn into this. Brutal shame and regret was followed by tears and apologies, but still it would continue to happen because I simply could not see it coming or control it when that wave hit me. I remember once being at one of my best friend's houses. Ted was a couple of months old and Harriet was playing up. I did my best parenting warning along the lines of "If you carry on behaving like that, I will take you home", before she inevitably did whatever it was again and my word was put to the test. Asking my friend to keep an eye on the baby, I swept H up and wrangled her into her car seat, her screaming and crying and me trying desperately to hold my shit together. The distance between our homes was only about five minutes, so I decided to carry through with my threat and started to drive the short journey home. Now, we know that being confined within a car with a screaming toddler is testing. Your ears feel like they might bleed, and your head feels like it might fall off, but those with a healthy mind would just swear under their breath and keep the end goal in sight. However, this general and acceptable approach was unavailable for my brain to access in this instance, instead opting to join her in becoming a total, irrational twat.

For every breath that she took and screamed at me, I screamed back. For every tear she shed, I also shed one. She was saying something along the lines of she "didn't want to leave" and she wanted to "go back" and I responded with something along the lines of "Well, I didn't want you to behave like that. I didn't want to be ignored and I didn't want to leave either, but you gave me no choice but to show you the consequence of your behaviour", followed by us both just screaming at each other. Honestly, I screamed like I was two years old and had been told I couldn't use my favourite toy. We arrived home to find my husband in the kitchen. He took one look at me and the state of our almost-hyperventilating eldest child and just whisked her away to another room to soothe her as I collapsed onto the kitchen floor and wept. I sobbed and sobbed tears of shame, tears of confusion, tears of rage, guilt and regret. The shouting had stopped as my mind had collapsed. I had officially become the mother I swore I'd never be and had succeeded to scare my child. To say it was one of my lowest points would be an understatement, yet I look back on the incident now and try to reflect on what I did right, given that thinking about what I did wrong still makes me feel sick to my stomach.

I was crumbling rapidly, yet I refused to voice it or ask for help. On the rare occasions I would ask someone to help with the baby so I could sleep or get something done, I would feel sick with guilt that I'd put someone else out and disrupted their day, just because I couldn't handle my own shit like I believed every other mother was doing. I had winged it well through parenting so far, so why was I failing now? My mother-in-law suggested I go and speak to my doctor, and since I was at the end of my tether, I agreed.

Diagnosis

The appointment was hazy. All I recall is sitting in the waiting room with tears pricking my eyes before sobbing on his desk moments later. He asked me to tell him three things I felt. In a nutshell, my issues were:

1. My overwhelming guilt towards my kids, my husband and myself.
2. I felt achy and sore in every joint of my body.
3. My thoughts were unclear as if they were covered by a veil; one which was holding them back from the forefront of my brain and stopping me

from being able to articulate what I wanted to say. I couldn't even concentrate enough to think about the words I wanted to use.

He diagnosed the obvious – Postnatal Depression – and I wasn't shocked at all. In fact, I was relieved to have an answer and to be able to finally admit to people how I was really feeling and have an explanation for it. My fear of saying it out loud and making it a reality had backfired and bit me right in the arse, because if I'd have just spoken up sooner, I could have saved myself a long recovery and missed far fewer precious memories that I will never get back. I could have enjoyed my boy a bit more. I could have smiled for my daughter a bit more. I could have had more support. Shoulda, woulda, coulda…

This mental illness robbed me of my joy and the very characteristics which made me myself at the very time that I needed them the most. Simple pleasures I would once relish meant nothing. Ste was shocked on one occasion when he gave me £100 to go and treat myself (something which prior to all of this would have been spent in less than half an hour on a lot of shit I did not need, but I HAD to have), but I returned four hours later and gave him the money back, stating I hadn't known what to get or what I was even looking at as I perused my once-favourite shops. Nothing seemed to matter. I was just empty. My head didn't work like it used to. I was a shadow of my former self; no effort, no energy, no smile, no fucks given. The only thing that powered me through each day was knowing that my children had to be washed, fed and loved, and I did my best to achieve that.

My once brag-worthy marriage was as strained as my mind and tired body. Sex was absolutely the last thing on my to-do list (my libido was zero), as was reassuring Ste that he still mattered. He had to watch as his wife fell apart and could no longer be the central glue that bonded us together as a family. Then, on top of that, he had to step up and pick up the pieces to ensure we survived it. He had to be both parents whilst I, although physically present to be an extra pair of hands, felt like a piece of useless old furniture taking up space and sentiment in what was once a tranquil, family home. Having said that, I never got to point where I felt they would be better off without me there. Quite the opposite. Despite my uselessness, I still thought that if I stopped trying to be 'Mum/Wife,' the house would fall apart; a notion which added to my anxiety, stress and guilt on the days when I was unable to achieve the household status I constantly set for myself.

My world, once bright and hopeful, just went dark. It was like somebody had flicked a switch off but hadn't turned it back on again despite struggling to see. I was like a broken lightbulb that nobody had bothered to replace (because let's face it, it would usually be me who would be expected to check the type of fitting, go and purchase the new bulb and then change it), because I wasn't there to do it as usual, so it just hung damaged and useless in its fitting. I was the lightbulb, and my filament was broken. Something that can be fixed or at least improved but requires recognition and effort to do so. I needed to find my dimmer switch, start it on low and gradually crank that shit up until it burned as bright as the sun.

Treatment

Upon my diagnosis, the doctor had prescribed me a course of anti-depressants, to be taken immediately and reviewed after a month. Stupidly, I listened to the judgement and inexperience of others when they said: "Ooh, be careful with those", "You can become addicted to those", "You don't need drugs, the pharmaceutical companies are just paid to push them", "Get some fresh air and more sleep". Those little life-savers sat for ten months in the back of my medicine cupboard as my 'safety net' whilst I attempted to self-heal through holistic and natural methods (gin, St Johns Wart and acupuncture).

After the unexpected and tragic death of one of our best friends from cancer the following autumn, I found myself at my rock bottom. God knows I had tried my best. Months had passed and I had genuinely done all I could do to improve my mental health, yet I was barely in a mildly improved state of mind than I had been at first diagnosis. Knowing that I had nothing left to lose and finally recognising that I needed further help, I began taking the prescribed daily dosage of the anti-depressants. And OH. MY. GOD…! Two weeks in, after pushing through the minor side effects of nausea and insomnia, alongside booking in with a mental health counsellor, I changed. Suddenly, the clouds began to lift and disperse. I could think straight and organise my thoughts once again. My smile returned more frequently.

The biggest test and realisation that I was on the right path was encountering behaviour from the children (both being arseholes simultaneously whilst I was the only parent at home to deal with the situation) which would have previously had me shaking on the floor, yet not only did I survive the incident, but I handled it too. I parented the shit out of it. Of course, I was totally winging it, but I bossed it and coped all on my own, without any tears (from me) and more than that, I felt proud and capable. Oh hello self-esteem, welcome back!

That time felt like a re-birth. As the medication gradually kicked in and my serotonin levels increased, I regained parts of myself that I had forgotten all about, parts that I had liked. Slowly but surely, the light crept back in and with every new tiny achievement, I felt more and more like my old self again. I was awoken. As my confidence and character returned, I had a new outlook on life. Things seemed much clearer than they ever had before. My time and health were precious. Moving forward, zero fucks would be afforded for anyone who was unlikely to afford me the privilege in return. I was going to live my life with my little family of four at the very centre of it. My beating heart and my senses. Never again would I question my own gut instincts or doubt myself without good reason. Likewise, I would refrain from all manner of things and people who did not add emotional value, pleasure or uplifting into my life. I was back with a vengeance and ready to make up for lost time with my children and my husband. Gutted that I'd missed my last experience of having a newborn baby and immersing myself in that crucial and awesome first year of growth due to my head falling off, I vowed that I wouldn't miss a bloody second of the rest of their lives. And I would return to being an awesome wife with 50/50 shared responsibility of adulting.

Talking therapy had a lot to do with the attitude change I adopted. When I finally grew the balls to sit down before my therapist, Jose, and spew out my issues, the very first thing she said to me in response was "I had two kids a year apart and it fucked me up". I instantly loved her. She got it. She understood the juggle and the hardship and the emotional and physical torment of expectations. Appointments with her on a fortnightly basis got me through each week until I was ready to gradually start spacing our meetings further apart, to a month between, then a couple of months, until eventually cancelling my appointment because I felt like I wanted to try going solo without her. She responded in such a way that filled me with pride and gratitude; that she "loved it when clients felt at a turning point to go and boss their life after some tough mental graft". I know she is still there for me should I ever need her safety net again. Therapy is a personal experience and one which should be tailored to the individual seeking it, but that shit works.

Sometimes, it is far easier to spill your deepest, darkest thoughts and feelings to a relative stranger than someone close to you, but you've got to find a mentor that you gel with. I have friends who have sought talking therapy for both minor and major mental health issues, and a few have continued to stay in therapy long after the turning point where they felt better, purely because it makes them feel good. It gives them the opportunity to find clarity and recognise improvements they make on a weekly basis. Therapy is never something to be ashamed of. It is a way of soul searching and getting to know yourself better. A good therapist is worth their weight in gold.

Onwards and upwards

So there you have in a nutshell, my own personal experience of suffering with AND and PND. I am proof that it can get better. As I write this, I am six months in from the day of starting medication and I have just weaned myself off it because I wanted to see whether I could cope without it, and I honestly feel okay. There are days when I struggle with my emotions more than others; noticeably around the beginning of my period when I once again return to raging-dragon mode for three days, but nowhere near the scale of my PND rage. Coping with day-to-day parenting has become easier; I can think clearly and logically about what to do when faced with a challenging toddler, and I have become much kinder to myself, learning to forgive myself in the moments when I do struggle or when I have to ask for help. I still lose my car keys and find them in the fridge, I still have moments when I walk into a room and can't for the life of me remember what I went in there for and I still have days where I'd rather stay in bed. However, my motivation and determination on those mornings are sufficient enough to haul my arse out from under the duvet and face the day with an attitude of gratitude and strength to overcome whatever may come my way, safe in the knowledge that bedtime is only ever several hours away, and tomorrow is always a fresh start.

The thing about PND is that when you think it's all over, it isn't over. A mental health issue is never really over. Even when you have 'recovered' from it, you have to learn to live with the repercussions and changes that occurred during that dark time and build a new normal whilst trying to forgive and find yourself again. Once you have experienced it, you can never go back to the old you again. Sure, you can find happiness again, but acceptance of the trauma that led you there is what spurs you forward to the next chapter. Only once you accept the fact you've reached the pit of despair and rock bottom, and you start being kind to yourself about it, can you take the baby steps to grow from it and hopefully stay away from it.

If you are there in the pits of desperation right now or you know someone who is, please take comfort in my honesty and reassurance in my words. Yes, it feels like the world is ending. You feel like a twat, and actually, you don't really care some days. I know you've forgotten who you were, but it's okay, you can recover from this and be better than ever. There are so many aspects of modern life which contribute to mental health disorders. All you can do is be aware of them and admit when you get caught up in it regardless of whether or not you can pinpoint the reason for it all unravelling. Ask for help. I beg you. Don't wait longer than you ought to, and please do not suffer in silence. You are NOT a bad parent. You are human. Your mind matters as much as your body. YOU matter. Do not be judged for taking medication or going to regular therapy and remember that nobody is living inside your head except you. You are the one that has to live with those thoughts and feelings, nobody else. It's okay not to be okay, mama. You might not have *got this* right now, but you can get it back.

5.

Marriage

Make or Break

It's a funny thing and feels strange to write about one's marriage in past tense, when in reality that marriage is still very much alive and in the present. However, it feels like the correct tense to use given that it's been seven years and two children since we said "I do", and we are in such a different place now. We are no longer that carefree and relaxed couple who kiss passionately and laugh daily. Although we are now getting back to that place, it feels like the next chapter is approaching. In truth, there are days when the only passion has been a heated argument and the only laughter is sarcastic scorn.

Marriage in my eyes is to devote yourself to one person only for the rest of your life, so it seems obvious to me that it won't be plain sailing throughout the many years you are together. I totally understand why the stress of having children can damage a relationship beyond repair. You're no longer 'just for each other' ever again. The world of 'me and you' becomes 'me, you and them', and it can rock you to your core if you don't see that coming, despite how ready you think you are. It's no use in thinking that your perfect relationship won't change. Believe me, we were that couple who said, "the baby will fit into our lives and become one of us and do all the things we like to do, and life will remain the same but enriched". It aint gonna happen. You can still be in love and attracted to each other with respect and humour, but that new addition did change our relationship. It turned it upside down, around and around, on its arse and then shot it back up to the sky day after day. It's a non-negotiable, mandatory, parenting sacrifice and you will sit there missing the 'us' you once were but thinking it is worth it just as I have.

We met whilst I worked behind the bar at a gym and he worked at the driving range next door. The staff from both places used to frequent the local pub in between them. I knew he liked me from early on, but I wasn't interested and used to roll my eyes when he'd swan into the bar ten minutes before closing time and order some food (just so he could see me). It took him seven brave attempts to get me to go on a date with him. The last time he asked would have been his last try, and I said yes just to shut him up, but as it turned out, we had the best time. I found him to be funny, kind and honest in a world where men rarely wear their hearts on their sleeve. Falling instantly, we kissed before I got out of his car on the return home and banged teeth. He thought he would never hear from me again, I thought it was an anecdote I would tell our children.

Our relationship was cemented over the forthcoming weeks as we would frequent the same nightclub in town then stop on the way home for a burger and a communal wee in the park, him aiming carefully at the wall in the dark whilst I squatted and drip dried next to him, laughing about the evening's events. He never splashed me once, God love him.

In his wedding speech, Ste poked fun about the type of person I was when we took those vows: "excessive spender", "over-sharer", "stubborn and headstrong woman". All true and valid observations and all stated with affection and love at the core of the tribute. In turn, my Dad teased, "Thank you for taking her off my hands, you're a brave man" (or something along those lines). They both got me spot on. I am stubborn. I am impulsive. I do enjoy a bit of luxury and I am certainly passionate about matters of the heart. It was the most blissful, happiest day of my life. At 28 years old, after eight fun-filled years together, becoming Ste's wife felt awesome. We'd bickered here and there along the way but nothing extreme, and generally speaking, we were the 'perfect' couple. We had each other's backs. We were best friends. There was honesty, respect and a great deal of humour, and although we were two very different people, often with very different perspectives on things, we held similar moral values and ethical beliefs. We both wanted children one day (Ste initially only wanted one), but we weren't in any rush to make that happen. To this day, we still agree that making the decision to terminate the first pregnancy when we had only been together a couple of months was the right thing for us to do. We had no regrets, despite it leading to us splitting up for six months whilst my head fell off until I realised how much I missed him.

Our twenties were epic. We spent our time between work and university in pubs and clubs, at festivals, in bed, or on the couch watching back-to-back box sets. We were compatible. We were so happy. I look back on my twenties with immense fondness and pride. A job well done, I think. I bossed that decade and don't regret a moment of it; I learnt the lessons I was supposed to and lived life to the fullest. In hindsight, the glory of my twenties is a massive contrast to the graft of my thirties. I simply did not have a single fuck to give, no children, no mortgage, no solid career. Just days in, nights out, enough money to eat and Ste by my side having fun. Twenty-something perfection. I often wonder how different life would have been if we had decided to keep that first baby rather than terminate the pregnancy. Would we still be together? Would we still be in love? Would the rest of my twenties have been as enjoyable? Would I have missed out on so many memories, or would they have just been replaced with different ones of a motherly nature?

In all honesty, I take my hat off to young parents as I imagine it's a tough gig, but maybe youth and energy lend themselves to making a more capable mother. Who knows? Does age even matter at all? All I know is that for me, becoming a parent in my irresponsible, immature, clueless twenties would have been a terrible move.

The Fur Baby

Not long after we first got together, we bought a dog, a Cairn Terrier puppy we called Alfie. Ste used to DJ a lot at night, so Alf was my company of an evening when I got to an age where I grew bored of accompanying Ste to the clubs; an age where my wiser mature instincts began to kick in and I started to see that environment for the fake and materialistic nothingness it was. I'd kiss Ste goodbye of a Saturday night as he headed out of the door with his tunes uploaded and relished the thought of star-fishing in bed with the dog. Of course, I missed Ste, but the thing we used to enjoy the most at the beginning,(getting shit-faced in clubs) inevitably lost its appeal in favour of boxsets and quiet, sensible evenings eating out. As long as he still enjoyed DJing, I had no issue with him continuing to do it. The extra income was appreciated, and music has always been his passion alongside golf. Somewhere towards the end of his twenties, he saw the game for what it really was and opted out, choosing to spend his evenings at home with me and Alfie.

That puppy was our first baby. He was bought without much thought or consideration to the responsibility of becoming dog owners and what it meant, other than unconditional love and something that we both had to keep alive and happy. I remember the day that we paid the deposit for him, taking a picnic and sitting on the hill at a park. We discussed names and were very much both on the same page with what we liked – something which was somewhat of a disagreement when I got pregnant. That furry little love spent fourteen glorious years as part of our team and brought us so much joy along the way. When I had my first baby, he greeted her with licks and wags, then when I had my second, he was far less thrilled as he knew once again he had to be knocked down the pecking order. Don't get me wrong, he was a delight with them both. He was such a kind natured and loving fellow, he took the mayhem in his stride, but I swear I had more parental guilt over him than either of my kids in his final years. He must have been miserable. He went from a quiet, peaceful home, being the centre of our universe to a house filled with noise, busy-ness and chaos in his old age at a time when he deserved rest, cuddles and respect, not a baby pulling his tail or a pre-schooler teasing him with snacks. Even now, a year on from having to make the decision to let him go due to poor health, I haven't got over him. I don't think I ever will.

Now, it makes my piss boil when people compare their pets to babies: "Oh the cat woke me up at five a.m. to go out, it's like having a baby", "That bloody dog ruined all my stilettos, it's like having an unruly child", "Picking dog shit up is worse than cleaning a baby's arse". NO. No it is not. Childless people take note: NEVER compare looking after a pet to taking care of a human child to a parent if you value your life, because there is a huge chance the parent you say it to could take a chair to your face, and if they don't, then they are certainly imagining doing so in their head. That said, our Alfie really did pave the way for us to become responsible parents. We lost a degree of our freedom when he came to live with us in that we would never again be able to leave the house for long stretches of time. We had to feed him, bath him, keep him warm and comfortable, and happy. But ultimately, all he ever needed was the same fundamental necessity that a child needs – love. And loved he was. We lost Alf in the summer of 2019, just two weeks before we received devasting news that one of our best friends was terminally ill. So, in the midst of this, as well as lingering postnatal, his life was never properly grieved or celebrated. He currently resides in an urn in my cupboard with my memory boxes and photo albums. His final resting spot under his favourite bush in the garden has been dug out and prepped ready for him when we are ready to put him there, but I'm not ready to let go yet. I still like to sit him on my knee and stroke his urn when I'm having a shit day and nobody is around. When I see him again, I'll remember to thank him for his unconditional love and the things he taught me, as well as apologise for the fact he went from number one to number three in the space of three years. Mum-guilt kicking in…

Arguments

In an age where social media tempts us to show off what we have, there are many tiles on my profiles depicting images of me and Ste, happy and laughing, standing strong, enjoying each other, supporting one another, but only if you look back about four years or more. Those pictures have become less frequent in recent years. Why? Because now our camera lenses are pointed at our offspring rather than at each other. That, and because when we do take a picture together, we look that knackered we instantly groan at the sight of ourselves and delete it. Scarce are the days of glowing skin, bright eyes and a cheeky snog with a beer in hand. These days, you're far more likely to see a picture of us lying in bed at 7pm, dark circles under our eyes that touch our knees and a pint of water to try and hydrate our pale, tired skin. It's not that the love got lost, more like we had to spread it thinner to cover everyone with enough of it. But as the months pass by and our children become more independent, it is multiplying again as we manage to find more time for each other. Love mitosis: the love cells keep on growing and multiplying and eventually (in the not-too-distant future), we will be full to the brim and overflowing once again.

When Harriet came along, we slid right into our joint parenting style. Albeit fairly helpless, Ste was great during my labour when all I wanted was to hold (squeeze until it went white) his hand. It wasn't until a few hours afterwards as I held my new baby whilst sitting on the chair in the room drinking tea and eating toast (post-delivery tea and toast is the BEST you'll ever have), that I got my first glimpse of my husband, the new father, as he sprawled across the double mattress that had been put out for us to rest, and snored loudly. What was that sound? I didn't think he had ever snored before, but if he had, it had never irritated me to the point I wanted to cover his nose with a maternity pad. Infuriating. Letting that minor annoyance go for the sake of new parental bliss and a man who had just stayed awake by my side through a lot of blood, screaming and vaginal destruction, I now also understand the irony of the saying 'sleeping like a baby'. I didn't want to sleep like a baby in those early firstborn days (they don't sleep). I wanted to sleep like my husband. The man who wears earphones plugged in to a white noise app on his phone to go to sleep causing him to snore his beak off and remain undisturbed by a crying baby in the night. It antagonises me only a fraction more than when he needs a poo and disappears for forty-five minutes "because that is how long it takes".

We decided early on that I would play bad cop and him good cop until she turned thirteen; roles which I am certain neither of us stick to. The problem is we never seem to balance which cop we are playing on which day, and when we do, the other always loses their shit over the way it's being done. We often disagree. For a couple with similar values and being in agreement of how we want our children to be raised, I never once foresaw the disagreements over parenting that would shaft us on a weekly basis. They have literally torn us apart at times. Like I said, we never used to argue. I think in ten years we only ever argued a few times. We bickered lots, but never anything of epic proportion. Man, that has changed since having children, particularly since having the second one. It's as though our ability to reason and compromise disappeared with our freedom. There have been three occasions that I can think of where one of us has genuinely almost packed a bag and left or asked the other one to leave.

The first for me was deep in the middle of PND, before starting medication and in a haze of sleep deprivation. I can't even remember how the argument started. I rarely can to be fair, but it escalated to the point of me almost throwing a plate at him before storming out of the house and driving down to Aldi car park to sit in the car screaming and biting the steering wheel as I wept hot tears of frustration.

The second is more recent, although I was unaware of it until I questioned Ste why he was being moody. Apparently, I had offended him by calling him out on the way he had spoken to me and Harriet, which led him to being so angry at me he nearly didn't come home from work. I never apologised. I said I was sorry for making him feel shit, but I stood by what I'd called him out for despite it being very out of character for him. Speak to your women respectfully, men, regardless of their age or relationship to you.

There was also a time, when my youngest was about six months old, that I seriously considered splitting. The atmosphere in the house was unbearable. We were both tired, stressed and felt unappreciated and unloved. It had come to a head over another minor argument about parenting techniques and who had the right idea, when I decided I couldn't face the tension anymore, but you must bear in mind that my mental state at the time was not good. I was not in a good place and was not myself at all, which in hindsight I think had a lot to do with my overthinking and over-sensitivity. I was at crisis point. It wasn't that I didn't love him anymore, of course I did, but I literally could not cope with the tension and atmosphere in the house, and I was worried the kids would be picking up on it. I felt anxious when I needed to communicate with him, as though if I asked him to do something or dared to question the way he did something, it would explode into a vicious argument or worse, resentment. Again, it is likely that this was mostly all in my head, but I couldn't see past the fog at that time.

Confrontation has never been my thing. Having experienced an emotionally abusive relationship in my teens, I have always shied away from any kind of animosity and bitten my tongue where I thought it could lead to disagreement. Not at all because I thought it would go that way with Ste, but because it just makes me feel so uncomfortable and uneasy. The number of times I keep my mouth shut when I want to question or constructively criticise the way he does something is unbelievable, but still I do it regardless. Choose your battles as they say. I don't see it as being weak or a push over. On the contrary, I see my ability to not call him a twat more frequently as a strength; I am a peacekeeper!

A frequent example would be his bloody gaming console. He is in his late thirties, yet still insists on playing an online game against total strangers (I would like to point out that most of whom are teenagers, although I know that many middle-aged men participate in this ridiculously childish pastime) as a way to 'unwind and relax'. Unwind my arse! He is probably at his most agitated and stressed when he emerges from the gaming chair, moaning about "that cheating, fucking game", yet he still insists on using it as a method to loosen up after a tough day at work. It drives me mad, listening to him waffle on to NOBODY (he doesn't use headphones to interact) and swear at his opponent, wasting time playing a fictional game whilst reality is happening around him under his nose. I don't understand how a person can get so irritated and let something that is not real affect their mood so deeply. It's virtual reality. It is a game. Why he thinks he can switch it on and play when the kids are around is beyond me. Not only is he denying them quality time, but he is absent from parenting and household support whilst he sits in a world of fake football and pretend zombie apocalypses. It's a solo activity. It should be utilised when he is alone and there are no other responsibilities to take priority, such as doing something productive to help tick off the never-ending to-do list of housekeeping, or when the kids aren't around. If the bloody device wasn't so expensive, it would have had an irreparable accident by now. It makes my piss boil I hate it that much, but I do understand that it's what he needs to do. It is his sanctuary. It just irritates me that his sanctuary is a place where he "can't press pause because I will forfeit the game". So when he's on it, he's on it without a pause until the bloody game finishes, which can last up to half an hour.

Granted, there are times when he also bites his own tongue towards me, but I reckon if we admitted it, there would be at least half the conversations we have in a week that would lead to a row if we let it. It's stress. It's sleep deprivation. It's mourning the loss of what we were and having to accept what we've become. As he once said, "It's not that I don't like who I am now, I just really liked who I was before too". It's grieving the old you to appreciate the new you. Grieving the old 'us' for the new 'us'. And it is a tough learning curve.

Now, back to that time of uncertainty, I confided my thoughts and plans in a couple of friends who told me that my happiness matters. They understood that I loved him desperately, but I wasn't okay with the marriage the way it was. I barely saw him; he started a new job when Ted was five-month-old which demanded his time and efforts away from home. He grafted his arse off and I knew it was for our benefit, to build a future for us as a family and support us financially as well as pursuing his ambitions. It was the worst possible timing for it to happen. Initially, I was on board and thought it was a great opportunity, but as the long hours crept in and I was left feeling helpless and alone, I did question whether it was the right move, something I voiced to him. I now know that during those long days whilst he built a business on zero sleep, his main concern was if I was okay at home alone with the baby, but in honesty I felt like a single parent. I would dread the bath and bedtime routine each night and anxiety would kick in around 4:30 p.m. as the hour approached when I'd have to deal with evenings by myself. Weekends were the loneliest time. Most of my friends, who don't have children yet, spend their weekends with their partners or families whom they don't get to see during the week; the last thing they want to do is spend their free time in my chaos helping look after my kids. Saturdays and Sundays spent solo parenting whilst you see images of families together on social media, parents having fun days out together with their children, or date nights without them, are torturous when you're stuck alone and already feeling shit.

I've always said that parenting is the only job in the world where you feel loneliness like a black hole even though you have another human stuck to you 24/7. You wish for company, yet when you have it you yearn to be alone and silent. That said, it is incredibly frustrating to have a spouse who talks all day for a living to the point that the last thing they want to do upon arrival home is talk some more and be talked to, when I've spent the day talking to the kids and cannot wait to vomit vocabulary to an adult.

I don't know whether it was sense or plain old love that kicked in, but I did change my mind and decided to drop the idea of separating. I knew I didn't really want to split at all. I loved him too much and I didn't want to imagine a future without him by my side and the four of us together as a family. He is my rock and honestly the most wonderful man, gaming console aside. Deep down, I know that he is an absolute star of a man and although I don't always like him, I am always in love with him. Always have been. Always will be. With every fibre of my being. He is essentially, in figurative terms, half of me, and I wouldn't be whole without him.

When I was diagnosed with PND, he slept in the spare room with Ted for six weeks. He did every night feed and early get-up for the entire time so that I could rest. He was incredibly supportive, but we both have our flaws; nobody is perfect. He likes to point out his good deeds in defence of a bad one. In the midst of tiffs, he will occasionally throw something back in my face in order to defend or justify his own behaviour, not out of spite or malice, but because he just doesn't see things the way I do. His defence mechanism in an argument is to ignore the thing I'm having a go at him for and bring up something totally unrelated that I do which annoys him. That's the problem with men, they are a completely different species. I've spoken to a great number of women who love their husbands dearly but cannot understand their weird ways. Let's look at some common examples:

Him: "Darling, I washed the dishes!"

Wife is thinking: *Well done you for washing the plate on which you have eaten the food I prepared you from. However, there are still specks of mash on the pan I used to make it, and the glasses are still smeared with finger marks.*

Him: (Switching on his Xbox) "I will fix that thing today with my man tools!"

Wife is thinking: *It's been sitting there for six weeks during which time you have said you would fix it 53 times. I do not hold much hope to see the thing fixed today.*

Him: "I can't do anything right according to you."
Wife is thinking: *No, because you do everything half arsed or with half the amount of energy and dedication I put it into it.*

You see, it's not that I am ungrateful for his efforts, of course not! I very much appreciate the times that he contributes to our to-do lists and I will nod along in encouragement, "Oh thank you darling", "Well done darling", "You're the best", in order to stroke the male ego. But the fact of the matter is that men honestly have no idea how much we actually do, let alone the capacity to copy it.

How many of us have managed to get that longed-for night out with our friends or a rare weekend away with them, expecting the house to fall apart in our absence but actually being greeted upon return by children still alive and a clean kitchen? We get lured in by the impressive display, pleased that the father has fathered well until we see the washing pile. And the ironing pile. And the skid marks in the toilet. And the rotting fresh veg in the bottom of the fridge which is there because beans on toast was consumed instead of broccoli. No wonder my kids think Dad is more fun.

The mental load of being the mother and wife tends to be incomprehensible to most of the male species. The things that we do beyond what they see as essential will never get the recognition it deserves, because to them we are all overreacting, overanxious, overthinking mentalists. They do not see the five things we do whilst we are on the way to the room to do the task that they know we are going to do. They do not recognise the sheer amount of mental to-do lists we compile in a day which are extended task by task as we go along so that things keep ticking over smoothly. Come on, we are all guilty of opting for a blow job instead of sex from time to time so that we have chance to compile our next to-do list for the following day (not every time, but definitely on occasion). All that they see is what is obvious to them – the black and white. The only grey matter they see is what we have the energy to show them in the bedroom if we aren't too knackered, and to be frank, that's what they are most grateful for.

Work and Time Management

Ste and I have had so many disagreements over how our time is spent during a week. He genuinely believes (and openly admits) that he works harder than I do. For the record, let's set this straight and jot down roughly what a part-time, working-from-home parent of two young children (me) does in a normal day:

1. Wake at the crack of dawn and take the baby downstairs (we do manage to split this fairly evenly between us depending on whom has had the shittiest night's sleep).
2. Make baby's bottle.
3. Prep baby's medication.
4. Make a brew for both adults.
5. Add baby's medication to his bottle after prising from his hands.
6. Change wet nappy.
7. Hand out brioche in the hope it will pacify them long enough for you to drink your hot tea or coffee.
8. Make cereal.
9. Clean spilled cereal fromthe carpet/couch.
10. Hand out more brioche and re-heat brew in the microwave.
11. Make toast.
12. Make more toast because you made it wrong (crusts were removed/it was cut into the wrong shape/they didn't want jam/they hate brown bread).
13. Eat your own toast with a toddler stuck to the other side of it gnawing at the best bits.
14. Re-heat brew again.
15. Tell children it is time to get dressed.
16. Chase children around the house like a sheepdog, using bribes to get them near the pile of clothes you have put out for them.
17. Endure abuse and a tantrum because they don't want to wear the clothes you have put out but wrangle them into said outfits anyway like cats resisting a bath.
18. Chase them once again with toothbrushes, toothpaste and a wet facecloth. Get screamed at for wiping brioche off their chins.

19. Brush their bed hair (if they have some) which looks like a burst mattress and attempt an 'Elsa' plait as instructed despite no bobbles in the house. (Where do they go?!)
20. Judge the state of your efforts so far and question whether or not they look fit to be seen in public without risk of being assumed neglected.

All that within around an hour of waking. It is at this point that if you're lucky enough for it to be a nursery or childcare day, you throw a hoody and jeans on over your own pyjamas, chuck on a bobble hat to cover bed head, use a baby wipe to get the sleep and yesterday's mascara out of your eyes and pop in a piece of chewing gum before herding them into the car for drop off. For argument's sake, let's continue with a working day so the offspring are out of the picture for a few hours, just to prove that our lives are not easy just because they are not in the house:

21. Return home, make a fresh brew.
22. Shower/brush teeth (always wash your hair on non-child days because you don't know when your next chance will be), dry hair and get yourself dressed. Shave your legs if it's summer and you can actually be arsed.
23. Check bedding in each bedroom – make beds and change sheets if necessary.
24. Tidy away children's toys etc from the morning chaos.
25. Wash children's toothpaste from sink and flush toilet which they left proudly for you to see the contents. They live by the mantra "If it's yellow, let it mellow".
26. Put a load of washing in.
27. Put the dryer on with yesterday's last load inside.
28. Wash pots from breakfast and wipe down kitchen.
29. Hoover toast crumbs from the carpet.
30. Check the calendar or diary to make sure there is nothing important happening that day which you might have forgotten.
31. Make a fresh brew and take to wherever your workstation is.
32. Try to ignore the ironing pile in the corner of the room and the open laptop.
33. Remove post-it notes with scribbles all over that your pre-schooler has left for you on said laptop as a gift.

34. Find a new pen because she has used the ink up in the one on your desk.
35. Work.
36. Lunchbreak.
37. Unload washing and put in another load.
38. Throw contents of dryer into ironing basket.
39. Work.
40. Avoid eye contact with your bed from across the landing.
41. Work. Use your brain to think about something other than domestic jobs around the house. Immerse yourself in something that makes you not 'Mum' for a few hours. Speak to other adults if you can.
42. Finish work and think about what to cook for tea.
43. Get your shoes on and go to collect children from childcare setting.
44. Realise you haven't got enough petrol to get there. Go and fill up. Get stuck in traffic.
45. Arrive late to pick up kids so that they're the last ones there and get a load of grief from them.
46. Feel like shit and promise them chocolate to make up for it.
47. Wrangle toddler into car seat who insists on seizing up like a wooden board and refuses to be bent into sitting position. Persuade pre-schooler into the car.
48. Return home and pick up discarded coats and shoes from the hallway to hang up.
49. Clean mud off the carpet.
50. Unload washing machine.
51. Make a brew.
52. Negotiate suitable pre-bath snacks with pre-schooler.
53. Cut up grapes.
54. Reheat brew.
55. Herd both children upstairs for bath time.
56. Undress them and put dirty clothes in washing basket.
57. Break up an argument over a toy.
58. Shout at pre-schooler for attempting to climb into the bath before you have checked the water temperature.
59. Step in a wet bit of carpet on the landing, remove your socks.
60. Clean baby's wee up from said carpet.

61. Chuck the kids in the bath.
62. Wash hair (far too many issues caused at this point to list, hope that neighbours do not think you are killing them from their screams).
63. Break up a fight over a bath toy.
64. Get toddler out of the bath, chase naked wet child with dry towel before they slip on tiled flooring.
65. Get pre-schooler out of the bath, argue over drying in-between their toes.
66. Herd both children into our bedroom for hair dryer.
67. Panic as baby falls off the bed (they're fine, just a bump, but you now need a gin).
68. Attempt to dry both children's hair at the same time.
69. Get baby into fresh nappy.
70. Pull out pyjamas and their clothes for the following day.
71. Realise that they have no clothes for the following day because you haven't washed/ironed them in time.
72. Raid ironing basket for something reasonably unwrinkled.
73. Get shouted at by pre-schooler because you picked the wrong pyjamas.
74. Get both kids downstairs, in pyjamas, in time for CBeebies bedtime hour.
75. Make bottle for baby.
76. Prepare medication for baby.
77. Pour a large gin for yourself.
78. Add baby's medication to his bottle after prising from his hands.
79. Try to calm down hyperactive pre-schooler, insisting that it is now 'quiet time'.
80. Make supper for children.
81. Clean up supper from carpet.
82. Change baby's pyjamas which now have cereal on them.
83. Add another ice cube to your gin.
84. Chop the veg for yours and husband's dinner.
85. Sit with children before the sacred 'Goodnight song'; *"The time has come to say goodnight... It's the end of a mental dayyy"*.
86. Turn the oven on to heat up for our dinner.
87. Usher children up the stairs to brush teeth.

88. Convince pre-schooler to try for a wee before bed.

89. Change baby's nappy.

90. Argue with pre-schooler that they haven't brushed their teeth for long enough, end up being forced to do it for them because you are anxious their teeth will fall out if you don't.

91. Attempt to prize baby's mouth open to brush their tiny teeth. Get spat at/dribbled on/snotted on/ toothpaste smeared on.

92. Chase baby into his bedroom, allow him to pick a story.

93. Wrangle him into sleeping bag and supply at least five dummies around the cot in the hope if he wakes he will find one without screaming you to find one for him.

94. Read story.

95. Kiss goodnight.

96. Get screamed at as you close his bedroom door and cross the hallway to pre-schoolers room.

97. Help pre-schooler tidy up toys which she has managed to spread across the room in the last five minutes of your absence.

98. Negotiate a suitable length story for that time of night.

99. Read story.

100. Tuck her in, kiss goodnight, leave room.

101. Go downstairs and put your dinner on.

102. Pour another gin.

103. Get shouted back upstairs by pre-schooler who needs a drink.

104. Go back downstairs. Sit down and pick up TV remote.

105. Get shouted back upstairs by pre-schooler who can't see in the dark despite having three nightlights on.

106. Go back downstairs. Sit down.

107. Get shouted back upstairs by toddler who has thrown all five dummies out of his cot and now regrets that decision.

108. Go back downstairs. Pick up gin.

109. Get shouted back upstairs by pre-schooler who wants to know why cows do not fly.

110. Use 'The Tone' to threaten them that they will miss a lovely activity which they are looking forward to tomorrow if they don't go to sleep now.

111. Go back downstairs and check your dinner.

112. Greet husband as he returns home with a grunt and a smile, because you have pretty much lost the ability to string a sentence together by this point.
113. Serve dinner for yourself and husband.
114. Watch mind-numbing reality TV so that you don't need to think about anything.
115. Wash up the pots/clean kitchen.
116. Both begin to nod off on the couch before calling it a day.
117. Brush teeth/wash your makeup off if you can be arsed.
118. Fall into bed.
119. Check social media for way longer than you intend to.
120. Agree to a quick blowie because you're too tired to make the effort to go on top for sex.
121. And sleep.

Guys, this is just one day out of seven and an example of the child-free workdays. I wouldn't have enough pages in the book to list all the things that go on in-between the activities mentioned here on a day when the kids are at home. It is mentally and physically EXHAUSTING, isn't it?! Even if you decide to have a pyjama day, a chill day with films or a general 'mummy-does-not-give-a-shit-today' day, the parenting is relentless. Your brain never stops. I would put money on it that Ste's workday, albeit long and tiring, is nowhere near as rammed as mine is, despite him being constantly busy working hard.

He rarely gets home from work and:

1. Puts a load of washing in/empties a load out.
2. Cooks our evening meal.
3. Takes it upon himself to do some ironing.
4. Gets the kids' clothes out for the next day.
5. Writes the weekly food shopping list.
6. Searches general parenting queries online.
7. Orders new shoes for the baby because his feet have grown again.
8. Orders the baby's repeat prescription.

You get my point. Their mental load is far less bulging than ours.

I feel like he has no idea how much I do to keep things ticking over smoothly. And unless you have arranged help and support once you have children, you are naïve if you think a similar routine will not apply to you. It's no wonder marriage changes with all this going on, where the hell are you supposed to find time for each other at the end of the day?

We have zero couple time. Well, maybe an hour (two at a push) at night-time when the children have gone to sleep, during which time we are likely to be found sat at opposite ends of the couch staring vacantly at the telly screen with dribble pouring from the corner of our mouths after a long day, or curled up into one another desperately trying to evade sleep so that we can enjoy being grown-ups together. In the four years since we had our first baby, we have had around five date nights. Five in 1,461 days! It had always been hard to find anyone agreeable to babysitting when we just had Harriet, then throwing a second child into the mix was like a repellent for any evening help we might have been able to sway with just the one. People were either scared or physically unable to look after two of them. I don't judge. I look after them both daily, and even I find the prospect of my two together for a length of time, a terrifying thought. However, it would have been nice to have been afforded the luxury of more evenings alone together in the early days of parenting. There were times when we were so detached from one another that we forgot what type of couple we had been. We often long for a break and imagine what we would do given the chance. Eat somewhere fancy? Go to watch a new film? Get disgracefully drunk and have sex somewhere obscure? (Very unlikely since the thought of parenting the day after a heavy boozing session is enough to make you go dry even on date night). Sometimes, we even go as far as to imagine staying at a posh hotel for a dirty night away. finding couple time has started to get better recently. We only ever get to go out alone with our friends; him on a boys' night or me on a girls' night. I love the rare occasion I get to dress up and put heels on (although it's that long between social outings that I forget how to do Out-Out makeup and worry I look like a transvestite), but it kills me that I don't get to go out like that with him by side. Likewise, he looks so fit when he gets ready to go out with the lads, I'm always gutted I can't stand next to him at the bar. But it is the way it is. It's either taking turns for a social life or not having one at all.

Now that we are out of the baby stage, one or two friends and family have offered to babysit so we should soon be able to enjoy being just 'us' again for a few hours, but we are lucky that we made it this far into parenting and are still married with the lack of together time we've had to manage with. As our childless friends begin to think about starting their own families and embark on their conceiving journeys, we are hugely excited to observe and support them, safe in the knowledge that when they are arse deep in sleep deprivation, weaning and holding their shit together, Ste and I may very possibly be in the pub having actual adult conversation whilst our cherubs are sleeping through the night under the watch of a willing sitter.

Sex

"I'll take the white lace thong and balcony bra with the silk stockings and the anal beads please, glamourous lady behind the counter at Agent Provocateur", said no mother ever. Seriously, Harriet is four now and I still own and wear knickers that I bought shortly after her arrival. My flaps are no longer coveted in silk, more like they are nestled inside a sensible cotton chastity belt, spilling slightly over the edges. Sure, I still have a kinky little lace number screwed up in a ball at the back of my underwear draw, but I'd rather go through contractions again than try to get my thighs in it. As for arranging the lace around my flaps and arsehole with a vulva that looks like Dumbo's ears tumbling over either side of the gusset, no thanks! Bridget Jones, although single and in her prime, had it spot on when she opted for those fucking enormous pants. Comfort over vanity every time these days. It's a rare treat for me to have the enthusiasm to venture into *Vicky Secrets* and rummage through the 'seven pairs for £25' offerings. It's usually when my period pants have snapped their elastic, signalling they are probably too worn and need updating. Ste sees that little pink bag and gets a semi-on, just for me to empty a load of black and white cotton briefs onto the bed. Poor lad.

A friend of mine who has three children and runs her own business told me recently that their three-year-old had almost caught her and her husband having a quickie in the bathroom one Saturday morning. Similarly, a magical queen who I follow on social media, went viral with a post about having a quickie with one leg up against the door to stop the kids coming in, and all I can think is where do they get the energy from to even attempt it? If I manage to escape from the kids for a few minutes, you're more likely to find me lying face down on the bed or hiding in the downstairs loo with a family sized bar of chocolate than inviting Ste to sample my goods. The baby notices if I even stand up from the couch, let alone try to go upstairs without him. He is rarely not attached to me, so just the idea of quick fingering is simply not an option in this house, although I understand that such activities probably do help to keep the passion alive. Simply put, there has been very little action occurring in our pants since getting pregnant with Number One.

I've never been a particularly sexual person. Don't get me wrong, I enjoy it when it does happen, but for me sex just isn't a big deal. I can take it or leave it and I'm slightly ashamed to admit that it isn't as high up on my agenda as it probably should be. It sometimes just feels like another thing I have to make time for in a world where there already aren't enough hours in the day, and I am exhausted during the hours that there are. We've had many a fall out over this; Ste often feels rejected and that he has to beg for sex, and I feel guilty for giving him that perspective. But I get where he's coming from. I never make the first move and I never make extra effort to spice things up. I'm just TOO TIRED. To me, lack of sex in the relationship isn't a game changer, it's just an inconvenience. I'd love to feel more energised and rip our clothes off for steamy passionate sex more often, but it's something I hope will return in time as the children are less reliant on us and we get more time to ourselves.

On a similar note, I did make the decision after having both children not to go back to hormonal contraception, I just felt so much better physically without it; my monthly headaches stopped, my skin cleared up and my weight stayed the same, so I figured with my PND hormones already raging, it was best to stay away from pumping anything additional into my ovaries. After giving birth, when you decide that you're ready to ditch celibacy, I strongly encourage you to think carefully about a contraception method that suits you. I'm trying to persuade Ste that it's his turn to take one for the team and get the snip, but my efforts are proving long-winded in getting him to book an appointment. (Must we do everything for them?!)

Speaking of effort, who is with me on the 'no shave from October-March' rule? Autumn appears along with jeans, tights and long dresses, and I am overjoyed at the prospect of not having to routinely trim my bush. By the time Spring comes back around, Rapunzel could discreetly house a tower in my pants and unravel my plaited pubes to the ground for her prince to climb up. Simply locating my clitoris amidst my lady garden is a task and a half, yet my husband insists men do not really care about the foliage, as long as it's clean and they still get to venture inside its wiry warmth (coming from the man who dutifully attempted to shave my bush with his beard trimmer under my instruction when I was heavily pregnant). But those who are with me on this will also understand the daunting task of hair removal at the end of the season, when it becomes necessary to de-fuzz. It takes you an hour and at least two razors or a very apologetic wax appointment to tidy things up down there. When Harriet was around two years old, she once stood with me in the shower, and as I lathered shampoo into my hair with my eyes closed, I wondered why she had suddenly stopped talking at me and gone quiet. I rinsed the soap out of my hair and glanced down to find her cupping her hands underneath my crotch and catching the water as it cascaded from my untrimmed pubes which had grown longer than I had realised. I also have a friend whose baby son used to point at her pubic hair and bark like a dog. So ladies, next time you take your poppet to the local swimming pool and worry about the spider legs protruding from the gusset of your swimsuit which you did not have time nor energy to trim that morning, have no embarrassment, we are all in the same boat there, and apparently, men don't actually care.

Sleep Deprivation

As previously mentioned, this unavoidable curse is a killer, and the effects it has on a relationship are savage. I lost count of the number of arguments we have had about who got the most sleep, who is the most tired, and who woke up the most times the night before, after the first fortnight of parenting. It's got to be one of the most prolific sources of disagreements that couples with young children have. It's always fuelled by late nights, early mornings, nights spent desperately trying to drown out the sound of a baby crying before you lose your mind, and a knackered body that is only just able to hold you upright on your feet. Given that both of my children were bottle fed, we always managed to share the night feeds, but the strain of a mother breastfeeding and a partner being unable to help out there must add to the torture.

When Ted was still very little and his reflux undiagnosed, Ste would often take him out for a midnight drive in an attempt to get him to stop crying and fall asleep (in hindsight, it was a rubbish idea, because the position of the rear facing car seat aggravated his reflux), whilst I remained at home drinking wine and wondering when the fuck I would ever get to sleep again. So many hideous mornings and days followed the sleepless nights that it was inevitable to be the number one cause of rows between us, but deep down we both recognised that we were in it together. We both had to crack on with the next day of work, and parenting in a haze of unexplainable tiredness whilst at the same time trying not to bite each other's heads off at the smallest thing, is a huge effort.

Also worth noting here, is that the mood we wake up in after a terrible night's sleep can easily determine the mood of the entire house for the day that follows. Frequently, one of us will begin the morning in a tired and defeated mood such that it is impossible to ignore the shift in atmosphere in the house. Now, I hold my hands up. I am not completely innocent of this – especially in my PND days – but I do try to make an attempt in the morning to start the day with a sense of positivity and cheer (after my first brew; I can't function without at least one hit of caffeine). There are mornings when shattered Ste sits on the couch, desperately adjusting to the daylight as the children change from 'sleep mode' to 'high-functioning, relentless energy and bickering' mode in just a matter of seconds. These instances have the ability to shit on my morning pancakes quicker than running out of gin on a Saturday night when Tesco has already shut. As time has passed, I like to think that we are generally more aware of the effect our moods have on the house and the kids' ability to read and take advantage of that. I totally understand and empathise with the shitty, early morning despair when all you want to do is crawl back under the warm quilt and ignore adulting. But I also recognise that seizing the day and making a conscious effort to set your attitude to one of *This is shit, I am knackered, I do not want to go to work, but I can do this, and I can attempt it with a smile on my face and some humour* is key to maintaining some kind of calmness and enjoyment from your day; a memo some men seem to have missed from what I am told.

As Harriet turned four and Ted began to sleep through at almost two years old, we treated ourselves to a new bed to celebrate the 'sleeping through' milestone, although we still don't get half as much time in it as we'd like. Quite often, one of us sleeps in the spare room because the other is snoring or coughing. Equally, morning cuddles (spooning whilst I ignore the morning glory poking me in my lower back) between us are often disrupted by Child One insisting she gets in, or worse still, one of us gets kicked out and replaced by her because she has had an accident in the middle of the night. Yes, sleep deprivation is the number one passion killer in our house for various reasons, mainly because without a decent sleep, neither of us can deal with the other's shit.

Love always prevails

Despite the unforeseen effects that becoming parents has had on our marriage though, I can sum up this chapter with an air of positivity for those of you who need to hear some gentle encouragement; love always prevails. Regardless of how much you think you hate each other in those dark moments of resentment, never ever make any rash decisions on the future of your relationship. These life altering arrangements should be considered and communicated over time. What seems like the end one day can feel totally different the next if both parties involved truly want to make it work. Talk, discuss, hold back on the sarcasm and judge the timing of your criticism. Listen and compromise.

The longest an argument has ever lasted between us is five days (one of actual words and four following days of defiant silence until someone broke), and I can't even remember what it was about now. Things do pale into insignificance when you look at the bigger picture; actually, you are in love and you can make this work if you work together. We are proof that you can get through it if you want to. There have certainly been times when we genuinely thought we weren't going to make it. Having said that, as I mentioned earlier, it seems completely obvious to me why some relationships don't make it. This shit is hard on you as an individual. To care so deeply about an extra person as well as yourself and your child/children too can be too much if you're not getting the same devotion in return from that other adult. But try to remember that it took both of you to create your tiny human. You may not always see eye to eye in respect of parenting styles, and that's okay, because whether or not your love for each other remains strong or you realise that you'll be better parents if you go your separate ways, you will always share the most incredible thing; your child. I credit the 2020 COVID-19 pandemic with renewing our love for each other. I genuinely thought that being quarantined in the house with both kids and my husband would lead to divorce and the kids being listed on eBay, but the reality was a far cry from that, and it was as though we actually came together as family unit and ENJOYED it. Who would have thought? Ste and I proved ourselves to be the ultimate team. We found ways to support each other, respect each other's need for space and time, and bring humour and fun back into every day, whilst realising that the two kids we made are ridiculous mini versions of ourselves to be worshipped.

The gin to my tonic

He may snore through the baby screaming.
  He may take 45 minutes to have a shit.
  He may not know how to cook or work the washing machine.
  But fuck, I love that man, and I'm so glad we made it through to the other side. There is nobody else on this earth that I would rather ask to shave my pregnancy pubes, compare grey hairs with, argue over not what was said, but how it was said, and laugh at the state of our lives with.

6.

Family and friend support

Find your tribe – mum mates

Being one of the first in my friendship group to fall pregnant was a challenge in the sense that I didn't have that pre-existing network of mums I could go to for advice and questions. I didn't have that person I could ask those first all important questions to: *why are my flaps swollen? Why the discharge? How do you deal with constipation without pushing the baby out prematurely?* At first, I relied solely on words of wisdom from one of my sisters, who at the time had her own twelve-year-old and seven-year-old, but had also been in a similar boat when she had her first child at twenty-three. I was almost thirty-one when I gave birth for the first time and had to transition from a life of carefree boozing and spontaneous holiday breaks to becoming Mum. Upon announcing my pregnancy to family and friends, naturally everyone was stoked for us, yet I felt an immediate sense of isolation from the lives we had been living as a carefree couple. I was lucky enough to have a best friend with a daughter six months older than mine. Although they are very different children – mine being the loud and lairy feral one and hers being chilled and spiritual – our children love each other like siblings. They are close but have the potential to bicker and fall out at the drop of a hat. During pregnancy, I would lean a lot on my friend as she understood the unexpected trials and tribulations that came with having a bun in the oven. My other reliable fountain of knowledge was my close friend and mum-of-two (now three) boys who speaks as I do; raw, unfiltered and between the two of us, completely open and honest about all things child related. These women are the reason I survived my parenting journey in those early days.

I am not the type to do baby groups or make friends via parenting apps. Slightly socially awkward, I do find it difficult to make friends in the first instance. I am relieved when people start conversations with me and it flows easily, so I have tried the apps as a way to extend my tribe and find other mums who articulate the same way I do, but the profiles of other parents just didn't seem to match my own parenting style, and it is so hard to sort the real from the fake on those statuses. I don't have the time nor the energy for bullshit or dampening down my words or feelings. I also tried a couple of baby groups (baby sensory, baby massage…that kind of thing), but I found it so hard to concentrate on not letting the baby put the things in her mouth (a quick spray with Dettol does not a sanitised toy make), and holding a conversation with a new person, given my newly appointed mangled mum brain, that I gave up fairly quickly. I accepted the fact that although my tribe was out there somewhere, I would find them in time. There were a few online groups recommended to me which I joined in the hope of finding like-minded mums, but I lost time to read or post answers to the constant updates.

Somewhere amongst the early days of Ted's reflux, another angel was brought into my life by way of a mum friend I had known years ago but lost contact with, yet we both followed each other on social media. Her son was only a few weeks older than Ted and also had severe reflux. She had been diagnosed with PND and her husband worked away a lot, so she understood the barriers in my life because she was experiencing much of the same. It took us months to arrange meeting face to face, but to find someone who completely got the space I was in with no judgement or expectations made such a difference.

Mum friends fucking rule. I still don't have many of them; most of my friends still don't have their own children yet, although a few have recently begun following me down the path to parenthood, and there have been a couple of announcements which I cannot wait to embrace, but the ones that I do have I hold very dear. We can laugh together and cry together. We can share anecdotes and roll our eyes in utter disbelief and dismay as to how much our lives have changed due to these tiny, demanding little dictators, but also how much we still love them despite the fact they did a shit in our slippers yesterday. We appreciate the need for a well-stocked gin cupboard, but most of all we have the knowledge that we have got each other's backs no matter what.

This gig is hard. It's the toughest job any of us have ever had to do and we support each other through it. No topic is off limits; we can openly discuss anything and everything from periods, to poo, to fuckwit husbands, to frustrating kids. We go off on tangents about shattered pelvic floors, body hair and everything else in between. It is a glorious mix of open questions and truthful answers. I genuinely wouldn't know who else I could share such things with. It's insightful and hilarious, and it makes me feel normal.

With both of my children in childcare, and the eldest approaching school for the first time, I am confident that my mum tribe will increase as years pass by. I will sniff out the like-minded ones and together we will support and watch our babies grow to be adults. For my close friends who want children in their future but aren't quite there yet, I will welcome them with open arms and a stiff gin when they join the club, finally able to appreciate the graft and joy which comes with it. I will love their children like my own, and in those moments where they confide in me that they feel they are being pulled under by it all, I will be there to provide relief in any way I can, because I know what it is like. I get it. Likewise, I appreciate how much mild resentment can be stirred up watching your childless friends' Instagram posts of their easy, relaxing weekends. It's easy to get frustrated at their lack of gratitude for a blissfully indulgent and spontaneous life in which they only need to think about themselves, but I've learnt that as much as I want to smack them sometimes for rubbing in my face without realising they are doing it, therein lies the exact answer. They don't know. They aren't doing it to piss you off, they are just sharing their life with you as they did before you had a child, because it isn't them who changed; it's you. Just like you do with your husband because you love him, you have to bite your tongue with childless friends when:

- They tell you they're tired
- They say their house is a mess
- They upload photos of themselves doing absolutely nothing on a Sunday
- They complain about their gorgeous, toned, tanned bodies
- They complain about the responsibility of workload.

You've got to let that shit go, especially with the friends worth holding on to; the ones who when they do eventually have their children, will join your club of gin and crying, and complaining and yawning, and soft-play loathing. Resentment and bitterness towards your mates will only make you feel more shit and isolated. If necessary, mute the group chat for a bit. Delete your social media app. Do anything that means you won't sit there fuming at their right to enjoy a peaceful life, because that isn't fair on them. But at the same time, bask in the knowledge that one day they will join you and finally get it. Their day will come. They too will spend their weekends in sweatpants covered in yoghurt, having had five hours of broken sleep, forced to endure eye to eye contact with a toddler whilst they have a poo, so close you can smell their mini cheddars breath because they aren't sure whether it's a "wet one". They too will be unable to venture out for date night with their husbands, by which time, you'll be getting a full night's sleep and a shower every day again.

This huge club of women in the know, with our collective saggy tits, stretch marks, shattered pelvic floors and eye bags is quite literally the most empowering group of females. It blows my mind that I never knew it existed until I became one of them. Find your tribe, love them hard. And if like me, you're finding it difficult to further your reach of them, trust that we are here. Just linger down the supermarket alcohol aisle a little longer and you'll see us. We know. We get it. There is a mum out there who is just like you. We all go a little crazy sometimes!

Grandparents

My relationship with my own mother has changed since having children. We used to be incredibly close, but recent events brought to light for me that although I was raised in a happy house, her parenting style is not the same as my own. She loves her children and grandchildren but isn't around as much as we'd like her to be. My parents have been married for over forty years and there is a fairly large age gap between them, which means that my dad cannot do certain things with my kids, like playing energetic games and the likes. They spend about a third of the year three hours away in their second home across the Scottish border, yet their primary dwelling and my childhood home is about a thirty-second walk away on the next street. You'd think that given their close proximity that we are one of the fortunate couples who get regular nights off and breaks from the kids, yet I refer to the five dates in four years as fact.

When we announced to my parents that we were having our eldest, they were happy for us, but the very same day as my mum and I walked the dogs that evening, she told me, "You do know that we are not *those* kinds of Grandparents, don't you?" Given that mum and I were so close prior to my pregnancy, I refused to believe it would happen, yet over the years we have drifted due to absence.

Mum was there to support me when I asked her and helped in ways such as cleaning my bathroom, ironing for me and changing my bedding, but fourteen days after I had my first baby, she went three hours up the motorway for the best part of a month and I was left reeling. My vagina had just exploded and there was a brand-new, crying human that wouldn't sleep in a basket next to me which I had no idea what to do with, "but honestly Mum, I'm fine".

I can't lie. I expected more support. Was that selfish of me? Perhaps, but I needed my mum, and I didn't feel as though I should have had to ask. I thought it would be a given.

For the last four years, my parents have continued to travel back and forth to Scotland for half of the year. I don't resent them for having their own lives and spending time in the place that makes them the happiest, really I don't. I just wish that the place that made them happiest was home with us. I wish they would want to soak up every moment of their rapidly growing grandchildren. I wish that they would see that Ste and I need time together to keep our marriage strong. I wish that they would realise that it does not need to take two days prior to a three-hour journey up the motorway to their second home to pack the car with their belongings; time which could be spent with family before my children forget what Granny and Grandpa look like for a month at a time. It makes me sad for them to be missing out, especially given that when my mum does have them, she is amazing at it. The kids adore her. She has that magical Granny quality that envelopes them in a love nobody else can provide. It felt as though, after having Harriet, she viewed our previously extremely close relationship as over, like she'd changed the rules and dynamics based upon a belief that now I was a mother myself, her job had evolved to a different kind of Mum role. Or at least, that was how it felt. Now we have two young children, things are more or less the same. She is on the phone if I need her but not always available in person. She will happily take my ironing for me if I ask, which I massively appreciate, but the offer to give us a break has yet to happen. She will only have one child overnight and that is only in an emergency. The last time she did this was when I was in hospital giving birth to Ted eighteen months ago, despite them both now sleeping through most nights.

My assumption is that she doesn't feel she can look after my kids on her own (I know my Dad can't really help at all), and I agree they are tiring and hard work, but she's never actually tried. She knows some of the struggles

Ste and I have faced, yet the suggestion that maybe a bit more quality couple time would be good for us seems to go unnoticed. I guess what I'm trying to say is that I am exceedingly grateful for every bit of help we do get from my parents, but I am overwhelmingly disappointed that we don't feel like a priority to them.

I have said all of this to my parents' face to face, so none of my thoughts and feelings about the situation would come as a surprise to them. I got to a point of enlightenment where I realised that by repeatedly expecting more from them, I was repeatedly setting myself up for disappointment, when in actual fact if I just stepped back and removed myself from that situation then I would be more content with the dynamics, which I am. Our relationship is in a good place now.

As children (even adults), your mum is the first person you turn to when you need something. It's a natural reaction for someone like me who had a good upbringing with my mum around. I love my Mum and Dad dearly, and I really enjoy the odd little catch up we have, or the times when they do have one of the kids, but it's fair to say that the bond between us has shifted and things are different now.

The in-laws

My husband's parents on the other hand, are a totally different kettle of fish. They have been our constant since having children, given that they live and breathe their kids and grandkids. So why don't we get more breaks whilst leaving the kids with them? Because my mother-in-law was diagnosed with Parkinson's in the same week that I found out I was pregnant with my first. Incidentally, it was also the same week I turned 30 and Ofsted were at the school I worked in; it was a very heavy week, and I couldn't even drink. This cruel bastard of a disease has robbed us all of the Nana she desperately wants to be. On her good days she always offers but can't really manage for more than a couple of hours with one of them, and that is dependent on my dad-in-law being around too. It kills her. She hates that she can't do it. Ste's older sisters had their children a few years before her symptoms started to appear, so she feels guilty that she can't offer us the same amount of help she did to them. This is something which we obviously have never even questioned, but it drives her own emotions. My in-laws don't seem to realise how grateful we are for the support they do give us when they can, especially given their situation. There are horror stories in abundance about unlucky women who got married and gained the in-laws from hell, but I am incredibly lucky not to be one of them.

Nursery

Oh where do I begin with this glorious respite? As you have probably guessed, I am not the type of parent that would rather stay at home raising my babies seven days a week. Despite being anxious when we first began looking at nurseries, I couldn't wait to finally get some time back to myself (albeit to work) and have some time off from being 'Mum'. Harriet was around eight-month-old when we took the childcare plunge and we never looked back. After a ropey start, which involved us moving her from the initial nursery we chose to a different one down the road, I can now safely say that as her learning journey began, so too did my path to finding my way as 'Helen, the working parent'. Those first eight months were a delight, but I embraced the freedom that nursery gave me like a celibate prisoner newly released from jail on his way to a brothel. Like every parent, I bawled my eyes out when I dropped her off for her first full day, but the drive home was epic as I realised that I was about to shower in peace, eat a full meal without sharing and actually spend a whole day doing something for myself and working. I have relished every single nursery day since. The staff at the one our kids attend are incredible and have become like extended family to us. They've supported and helped us through some dark times more than they will ever know. Our kids adore them, and we are so lucky to be able to drop kick our cherubs through their door at 07:30, three times a week (best feeling ever on a Monday morning), safe in the knowledge that they will be happy and well looked after. Ted was much younger than Harriet when he started there, only four-month-old, but we needed the break and space for ourselves. It was a tough decision but because we knew the staff so well already, we didn't feel too much guilt. Aside from the educational and social benefits the children get from attending, nursery allows Ste and I time to be just be ourselves without the kids. Granted, we are both usually working when they are there, but honestly, the routine has given us that extra bit of independent time without an ankle biter attached to us. I can put my makeup on and choose an outfit that isn't leggings in the knowledge that it won't be covered in snot by 10am. I won't be asked to open bags of crisps three times a day, and I don't need to occupy growing minds with glitter crafts and stickers, I can be an adult doing adulty things on my own.

Nursery gave me back a sense of independence, some self-appreciation and most importantly, my identity as an individual again. The thought of Ted leaving for school in a couple of years and losing some of those women from my life makes me feel a little lost and sad already.

The best advice I can give you on the nursery Vs home scenario is to put them in when it suits you and them. Whether they are 4 months old or 3 years old, the reason you choose to go down that route is nobody else's business and a good nursery wont question it anyway. There is a reason the baby staff are trained to care for children from 12 weeks old in most places. You don't have to feel like you should be keeping them at home and planning a plethora of educational activities each day for you to be a good mum. You're entitled to find yourself again, and if putting them in nursery is the way forward in order for you do that, then pack those nappies into their rucksack the night before with a spark of joy that you'll get your morning poo time all to yourself.

The judgy bastards

It goes without saying that for every two people you decide to invite into your inner circle, there will be a third who insists on attempting to drag down your mental state, usually without even realising that they are doing so (the Dorises and Harmonys). The ones who like to give you their opinions and 'constructive criticism', despite you not having asked for it, or not actually giving a shit about it. They like their voices to be heard and they enjoy feeling like they're a part of YOUR journey because they think they imparted some maternal wisdom. It isn't necessarily as simple as these kinds of women just being obnoxious rude bastards, sometimes they genuinely think they are just being helpful. However, if I've learnt anything from these ones, it is to develop a thick skin to judgement.

Those annoying, judgy eyes can hit you with their shitty, judgy lasers anywhere: the school playground, the supermarket, the park, the restaurant, even in your own home if you let your guard down and invite them inside.

They will spot you in a predicament and make assumptions about the situation, usually with an audible tut, an unhelpful suggestion or a phone call to an equally judgy mate to tell them what they have just witnessed. Fuck them. Let it go. What you have to remind yourself is that they have absolutely no inside knowledge as to what it feels like to be you. They don't know your children. They have not got a clue about your coping mechanisms, parenting style or how you choose to wing it, so their judgement is completely invalid and not worth stressing over. Likewise, never choose to comment on the way a mum friend (or any mum in general for that matter) parents her children unless you are asked to. There is nothing more frustrating to a parent than being told by someone they are doing it wrong. None of us have a fucking clue what we are doing really, so if you aren't asked for advice, keep it yourself. And when you are asked, deliver it honestly, empathetically and without a hint of judgement. Be kind, always.

It takes a village

Support as a parent is crucial for your mental health, your physical health, your marriage and your children. As the saying went back in my Nana's day, "It takes a village to raise a child", but these days not everyone is lucky enough to have access to a village. Many think they are doomed to survive this shit alone. Whatever your situation, I am here to confirm that you are wrong. Okay, on a physical basis, as in someone literally looking after your kids for a few hours so you get a break, you might actually be void of support, but on a despairing, complaining, over-whelmed with it all basis, NO ONE is alone. If friends and family aren't your option, go and seek your tribe elsewhere; sit in a local coffee shop with your baps out breast feeding, eyeballing every woman who passes you by in the hope they will be drawn to your maternal duty. Dare to join a baby group and even if you sit in silence, listen to the conversations around you and be brave enough to speak up when someone like you offers an anecdote. Tell colleagues your parenting truths, even if they are judgy non-understanding ones, because the gossip might spread far enough to attract Janet on the fifth floor, who is a newly single parent that can't do star jumps for pissing herself after an episiotomy and enjoys wine on a Friday night but wishes she had company. Be brave. Be yourself. Your tribe will eventually run over the horizon towards you like modern Bravehearts, ready to embrace you with their wild unbrushed hair, milk-stained pjs and bottles of prosecco lifted high like war swords, ready to welcome you to the fold.

7.

Me time

You can't pour from an empty cup

If I had a pound for every time I've spoken the words "I am a person, I matter too", to my children in the last four years, I would be writing this book from my secret hideaway mansion, in the middle of nowhere, in a place where nobody could ever find me, with a fully stocked wine cellar, a masseuse on speed dial and a fridge full of expensive snacks that I wouldn't open to find partially gnawed and put back in the wrong place. That is the dream; to be completely alone for 48 hours to please myself and not have to be responsible for keeping anyone alive other than me. What you don't realise when you become a parent, is the suffocating lack of personal space you become forced to endure on a daily basis. Any good parent thinks that it is important to naturally put their children's needs before their own, but what I realised was that there are occasions when this is total bullshit. There has to be a balance. One cannot go through a decade of life with offspring attached to your ankles, watching you on the toilet, speaking at you whilst you're trying to concentrate or demanding you stand in the kitchen and make endless snacks (which they end up not eating anyway), without some kind of resentment towards the fact that you are no longer your own person. You need space. You need time to eat, time to rest, time to think and time to enjoy the things that spark joy within you.

This chapter explores a few of the ways in which I have manged to capture the essence of myself; the things that I literally need in order to feel like a human person and an individual, not just Mum. So many women talk about losing their sense of identity when they become a parent. It's a natural reaction to the realisation that your life completely changes, and yes of course you do have to adapt with it to survive, but you don't have to ignore your own needs.

Me, myself and I

In the year of Harriet's first Christmas, my husband bought me a hotel room for one night. It was local, not over lavish but posh enough to have black-out curtains, a massive king-sized bed, a telly and a coffee machine. It was exactly the break from life I needed. My best friend booked a room for herself across the hall, and together we waved goodbye to our men and babies and fucked off in the car like Thelma and Louise on a 24-hour UK mini break. We had totally taken a shit-load of red wine and planned to do pedicures and facials whilst being young, carefree and off our faces for one night, but I think we both fell asleep in our own rooms by about 8 p.m. and met again the next morning shortly after my husband messaged me to ask if I could home because he had food poisoning. Furious, I slagged him off the entire way home for having made me miss the complimentary breakfast and return to reality early, but then I felt terrible upon seeing the state he was in upon walking back into my house. He was genuinely ill with Norovirus but had tried his best to leave it as long as he could before calling me so that I had the break I deserved. These mini hotel breaks became a regular feature in both mine and my friend's lives; we don't always go at the same time, but we realised how much the time alone meant to us and how much good it did us pressing the reset button.

Girls' nights out are always well received too as a way to blow off steam and just be myself, although the hangovers which usually follow them are enough to ensure they don't happen very often. Drinking mothers on a night off have the ability to clear a dancefloor and disgrace themselves like other women, and you are kidding yourself if you think an evening spent like this is a break. As fun as they are, they are just a temporary respite from reading the bedroom story and allow you to get shit-faced with your mates without guilt. The very first boozy night off Ste and I had together was at a friend's wedding in Palma when Harriet was five months old. (It's still the only trip we've been able to enjoy together since becoming parents.) We got so drunk that I was sick in a bin in the hotel room the morning of the wedding and nearly fainted from dehydration at the ceremony in blistering heat the next day. Note to mothers who have not yet dared to go boozing after having children: take it easy! Despite your excitement, you cannot drink the same amount anymore and will end up with severe beer fear the next day.

Music

There is something magical about music and the way certain genres or songs can instantaneously transport your thoughts to a time when things were less chaotic, and you were in a euphoric place. Everybody has that one feelgood song which uplifts the mood on the first few beats. I always used to listen to the radio in the car and enjoy the mix of music and banter, so I recently invested in a DAB radio for the kitchen, since this is where I seem to spend the majority of my time these days. When I bought it, I was thinking about getting back in touch with modern music – I couldn't tell you one song in the current top 40 chart if you offered me a million pounds to do so – so I thought at least this way I'd get my fill of tunes and also get down with the youth of today and what they are listening to. What a load of utter bollocks. The majority of what I heard that day was not music and hurt my mature ears (I am definitely old now and appreciate what I put my own parents through when I used to whack on the happy hardcore CDs in my bedroom as a teenager), so after a quick scan of the channels, I found the kind of music that makes my soul happy and now I can't stop listening. This might sound weird, but I enjoy the banter more than I enjoy the tunes sometimes. It makes me feel like I am part of an adult conversation, especially on the days when I am alone or with the kids and Ste is out at work. When I'm feeling lonely, it has a way of making me feel like I actually have company. I get my hourly news feed, brief enough to give me the vital headlines but not so long and in depth to send me under with information and facts, a bit of a giggle with the DJs and listeners who speak on air, and my fill of absolute bangers which make me slut drop to the kitchen floor tiles and grind my arse back up to the coffee machine like I am Rihanna. (That is, if she wore yoghurt stained t-shirts and slippers she had owned for three years.) There is nothing like the sound of music to mask reality for a quick fix of freedom.

Clothes and makeup

Working from home, people often comment on how lovely it must be to not have to find the time of a morning to get dressed up ready for a day at the office. I have no need for suits, makeup or even showering if I don't feel like it. However, this did become somewhat of an issue for me when it came to my mental health. As much as I would feel smug at nursery drop off that I could roll up sporting no bra and my PJ top under a hoody. (Nobody can ever tell – right?) I still can't help but gaze upon the super-mums who arrive looking immaculate in a well-fitted suit and heels with a full face of makeup and their hair perfectly tied up, brandishing two hyperactive children one under each arm, before ushering them into their nursery rooms and bustling back out to the car again to begin a work conference on loudspeaker. How the fuck do you guys do it? What is your superpower that allows you this kind of organisation of a morning and the motivation to achieve such high maintenance grooming? Mostly, I would return home from drop off, eat breakfast, shower and throw on something comfy to sit and work on my laptop. That would usually comprise of jeans and a hoody or leggings and a jumper, until one day whilst musing over these super-mums, I wondered if the crux of their power was how they felt when they presented themselves in such a boss lady way. It got me thinking; were the clothes I was wearing holding me back from productivity?

Even before I had children when I used to go out to work, I liked to make an effort with my clothes. I enjoyed feeling smart, washed and ironed and sometimes even trendy. I spent four years getting a 1:1 grade fashion degree for God's sake. It was once my passion. So I vowed to step away from the hoodies and only wear jeans with a nice top. And do you know what? It worked. Gradually, I phased out the loungewear and began to actually 'dress for work', despite often not leaving the house or seeing anybody other than the postman. These days, I save my hoodies and loungewear for sick days, or the days when I am generally just allowing myself to embrace feeling fucked all day. I swapped the hoodies for some cute jumpers and the leggings were replaced by tailored trousers and skirts which were suitable for both work and parenting making them good all-dayers from Monday through to Sunday. It sounds ridiculous but wearing a blouse underneath a jumper and putting my specs on is my way of informing the world I mean business that day.

On a similar page, I began to wear makeup again. Not every day, as I do believe it is important to let your skin breathe, but on the days when the kids are in nursery and I am bossing a full day sat before the laptop, I make the effort to put some slap on. Again, more often than not, nobody sees me, but the feeling of making the effort is enough to make me feel good about myself. I don't look in the mirror on my coffee break and think, *Jesus fucking Christ, you look like you haven't slept in four years. You need three of these homemade espressos as well as booking in your missed botox appointment,* and it makes me feel slightly more professional if a video call is required at short notice. The only thing about putting makeup on in the morning is having to make the time to take it off again at night. I'm a nightmare for going to bed in my makeup. Frequently, I just can't be arsed after brushing my teeth, and I just collapse into the bed hoping to wake up without blackheads or spots. However, as a fairly low maintenance woman, even I realised that as middle age approaches, wiping my face with a baby wipe just was no longer enough to clean my skin free of the day. Plus, I have already aged about two decades in the last four years (my frown lines are deeper than the Pacific), so I invested in some decent skincare products and got myself into a morning and night-time cleansing routine. It might not have knocked the last ten years off me as I'd hoped, but there is definitely a vast improvement and it does make me feel like I'm bookending the day with some self-care. Moreover, it's given me the confidence to leave the house and go amongst the public without any makeup on if I need to/can't be arsed putting it on, without having to worry about what other people think I look like. If anyone finds the actual fountain of youth though, please do let me know.

I am not your fucking slave

Personal space is a big one for me. By nature, I am a giver and a nurturer. I like to help, support and provide, but the suffocation of being constantly physically required really gets to me. I never knew that most young children are so clingy. Of course, you expect it with babies, but in my head I thought that as soon as children learn a bit of independence to do little things on their own, they detach from your ankles/knee/waist a bit, but this has not been the case with my own. If it's not the kids touching me, it's the husband, who enjoys nothing more than grabbing my tits at the most awkward times; frequently when I'm standing naked in the bathroom attempting to apply mascara. The children are on me ALL THE TIME; touching me, breathing on me, sneezing on me, climbing on me, pulling my clothing etc. As a hugger in general, you'd think I'd enjoy the physical contact, but it's like having two overactive large sloths using your limbs as branches whilst they claw each other off the territory. It makes me recoil sometimes and I do tell them off for using me as a climbing frame.

Self-care

I tried the meditation trend, I really did. Well, I tried it as much as my spare time would allow me to. The thought of being able to exist in complete silence for ten minutes a day held glorious appeal, but in reality, I couldn't find ten minutes to have a shower, so that pastime didn't last long. They say it helps to calm your busy mind and that it does take practise to get it right, yet I couldn't switch my busy brain off for long enough to see any benefit from meditation and on the rare days I did manage to complete the ten minutes without being interrupted by a child yelling "I've done a poo, can you wipe my bum", I'd spent the ten minutes with my eyes closed thinking what was on my to-do list for the day. Meditation isn't for me, although I do occasionally use the online apps to help me relax on the nights I struggle to get to sleep. I have friends who swear by meditation and the benefits that it brings to their mental wellbeing, who even attend meditation classes set in the tranquillity of actual lavender fields, so if this kind of self-care sounds up your street, I'd definitely recommend it. But if like me, you'd rather spend a rare ten minutes silence with a gin in a dark room, then maybe give that one a miss.

For me, there is only one from of self-care with a 100% success rate that's guaranteed to lift my mood and make me feel calm and in control. It's a controversial one. It's work. Writing is my jam. It's my happy place. It's where I can get lost in thought and words, using creativity as an outlet for my emotions. As luck would have it, I am exceptionally lucky to write for a living (for a company owned by one of my best mum friends), so the opportunity to switch off from the world and let my fingertips do the talking is presented to me on a daily basis. The sense of self-worth and achievement when I submit a piece of writing is like no other; it gives me a buzz, yet the physical action of typing is what really gets my juices flowing. It's as though whatever is going on in my life that day takes a back seat whilst I do what I do best. Nothing else matters. The crappiest of moods can be put on the back burner whilst I sit and work, using my brain only for joy and creativity. My job provides me with the headspace I need to feel like I've done something productive for myself rather than spending time doing something for someone else. Yes, it can be a challenge finding the motivation on the days following bad night sleep or those days when I really just can't be arsed, but it has the same effect on me as finding the energy to workout has on some people (not me – I loathe exercise); it always proves worthwhile making the effort. Not only does it usually tend to help clear my muddled thoughts, but it gives me a tremendous sense of satisfaction and pride in my own abilities as well as knowing it's earning me a wage. Daily circumstances and the kids may not always allow me to be the parent I want to be, but my laptop and keyboard never lets me down in being the colleague/employee I want to be. Time management can be an issue some weeks when there's a lot going on, but I've learnt to forgive myself on the days I don't meet the deadline I set for myself and make it up elsewhere. Life with children is so busy and I often find myself craving a writing session on a tough day. But punishing myself for not having an extra hour in the day is pointless, so I try my best not to stress out. I love what I do, and I know I'm incredibly fortunate to be able to say that. Work for me is like a habit that I never want to detox from. It's the place where I am not a mum, or a wife, or anything else to anyone else; it's where I am just Helen and my brain belongs to myself. It's my sanctuary. More than that, it's my therapy.

8.

Parenting

Expectation Vs. Reality

I thought long and hard about how to start this chapter. I eventually came to the conclusion that it doesn't really matter, because the information that follows will seem completely absurd to those of you who don't yet have children, yet it will ring completely true to those of you who do. Life with children is entirely fucking bonkers. There is no other way to say it and no point in sugar coating it. Your children will be the biggest headfuck you've ever had. You'll swing from adoring them in one moment to wondering how the hell you ever made such little nobheads. Your three-year-old will have the ability to make you laugh until you wee, then in the same breath, do something that makes you feel so frustrated you could put them on eBay. So I'm just going to pour a gin and jump in balls deep with the stark reality and a four-year trip down memory lane which already has my arsehole twitching.

Ask any mother what they miss most about their pre-parent selves and they will tell you at least one of these things:

1. Sleep
2. Free time
3. Personal space
4. A tidy house
5. Disposable income
6. Leaving the house quickly when going out
7. A social life
8. Her pelvic floor
9. Her tits
10. Having to keep only herself alive and well.

Rites of passage

These are the heart-in-mouth moments that every parent must experience in order to develop a well-rounded attitude to parenting. Most common incidents include:

- Baby rolling over and falling off your bed. Usually occurs within the first six months and leaves you more traumatised than them.
- Toddler pushing small, round food object up their nose/in their ear/into any other orifice which you then have to find a way to extract. DO NOT poke it further if you don't want a visit to A&E with your tail between your legs. But also, forgive yourself because you can't watch them 100% of the time and even if you did, they would still find a way to fulfil their burning desire of knowing what a raisin feels like inside their nostril.
- Bumping your child's head on the car door when putting them in the car seat. This can happen to the owners of any vehicle type. Again, it's an experience which is usually more traumatic for you than the child.
- Cutting a tiny, miniscule bit of their fingertip off when using the world's smallest nail clippers. This is horrendous. Expect tears from both of you followed by years of battles on a Sunday evening when it's time to check if they a trim at the end of the week. This can cause an aversion to nail cutting, that in our house we like to refer to as "Gruffalo nails".
- Poo finger: Schoolboy error – NEVER just shove your hand in the nappy without looking first, even if you've done the sniff test and it smelt okay. You will not be able to eat finger food on the same day, despite bleaching your nailbed.
- Reacting to disgusting habits, such as eating bogeys or belly button fluff. It starts with "OMG, princesses/princes don't do that darling, it's dirty!" and you stifling a vomit in your own mouth, but it eventually morphs into "Ewww go and wash your hands and don't ask for desert since you'll be full now". The vomiting in your mouth will stay with you every time.
- Public tantrums. Yes Sandra on aisle four, my child is punching the floor and screaming because I told her we didn't need to buy the Durex lubricant she mistook for bubble solution. Expect a lot of this and expect to leave your shopping half finished.

- A cutlery drawer full of pretty and expensive silverware taken over by a million Calpol syringes. Because they give them free in every box, and you never know what they will come in handy for.

Social Media

Where better to highlight the difference between the real and the fake than the holy grail of hashtags thrown around on the internet? To start on this subject, I will state an obvious fact: nobody's life is perfect. Nobody's. Our Instagrams lie. Regardless of what the *#blessed* crew are saying, even they aren't telling the entire truth. There is definitely something that they would change if they could, they just choose not to say it to the online public. I'm all for people being happy and loving their lives for sure, but we live in an age where this common misperception of an image in a little square grid showing the epitome of happiness is dangerous.

Frequently, I have felt below standard on the parenting front due to the flicker of an image or a sentimental hashtag most likely posted to inspire but sometimes just to show off. 'Sharon' from the NCT group appears to be bossing life; she washes her hair every morning, prepares three homemade meals from scratch a day, lives in marital bliss with her partner, enjoys family days out accompanied by photos where every family member is looking at the camera and smiling, dresses impeccably every day and spends her evenings with a delicious cocktail, sitting on a white couch in a living room so clean and tidy that even Mrs Hinch is envious. Bollocks. Nobody is this lucky. Hats off to Sharon, I mean it looks like she is living the dream. She portrays an image of calm and togetherness, showing her chosen followers that you can have it all and be euphorically happy, but what she neglects to show on her profile is the laundry pile that never ends, the argument she had with her partner last night because she couldn't be arsed having sex, the pile of dishes in the sink that she didn't have the energy to clean after she had cooked all day, the strain in her shoulders from carrying around a newborn that didn't want to be put down, the overflowing bottle bin, the stains on her cheeks after guilt-sobbing because she screamed at her toddler for refusing to lie down for a nappy change, the overdue bills on the kitchen counter, the unmade beds, the relentless burden of responsibility that plays on her mind when she stops trying to be SuperMum and takes a minute to herself to breathe; all the very real and very raw aspects of life which occur when you become a parent which Sharon chooses to hide from her public profile in favour of 'the good bits' which make her look like she is excelling. What she doesn't realise, is that the shit bits she doesn't show are the actual proof that she is bossing it. They are the challenges which she overcomes on a daily basis to be still standing at the end of the day. Everything else – the meals, the shower, the lovely trips out – they just are a bonus and prove only that she is able to push herself to a parenting extreme, which is not necessary yet hugely satisfying when it works out. That is why she shares those moments. It's her way of congratulating herself on being extra. Doing extra. She convinces herself that if people see those bits, they will think she is doing a great job at Mumming.

However, poor Sharon has not been told that she is still #blessed at the end of the day if all she has managed to do is keep herself and the kids alive and fed. You see, Sharon is not very kind to herself because she thinks that the opinions of people she doesn't even really know that well on social media matter. She would rather be judged on her ability to wear a full face of make-up and go the extra mile for her family, than her ability to tidy a playroom full of plastic crap and bang some chicken nuggets in the oven once in a while so she can sit and do nothing. She would rather people not know the strain that having children has put on her marriage because that's not fun, is it? That would be wrong, given that she longed for a family and as a couple, pre-kids, they used to be the Posh and Becks of the North. She has a reputation to uphold. And so many other mums look at her photos and read her status updates and think *Oh fuck off Sharon, you smug bitch.* A few might even think *Well done Sharon, you are the parent I want to be.* But what Sharon doesn't realise, is that by not being entirely honest, she has sent those readers spiralling into a thought tunnel of self-loathing and self-doubt.

But look at it from the other perspective; Sharon shares how shit her day has been and how much of a wanker her husband is, because he went to the pub after work for a couple instead of coming home to help, despite her messages telling him the kids have been arseholes all day. She shares an image of her unmade bed and her makeup-less face, holding a gin whilst the kids tuck into pizza for tea in the background. Suddenly, she has more likes and comments on her life in squares than ever before. Sharon has all of a sudden become relatable. No longer does she receive eye rolls and tuts from other jealous parents, but she receives messages of solidarity and positivity, encouraging her to keep going and hope for a better day tomorrow. Jenny from the NCT group who normally fucking hates Sharon and her bragging images of perfection has a lightbulb moment and realises that she actually isn't alone in feeling overwhelmed and swamped under by parenting life. Mary from NCT group, who actually rather likes Sharon and has always envied her 'shit together' attitude and persona, realises that perhaps Sharon might need a break and a beer away from her house, so invites her round for the evening. Becky from NCT, who is due in a fortnight stops shitting herself about meeting the expectations of and matching the efforts of the previous social media 'Sharons', thus allowing her to enjoy the last few weeks of pregnancy and become open minded and mentally better equipped for the journey ahead. Everyone who has consistently witnessed Sharon's picture-perfect outpourings of happiness and joy realises that she was only showing the best bits to make herself feel better, when, in reality she is just like most of us parents; extraordinary because she has the energy to give enough of a shit about caring what people think, yet miserable because she gives too much of a shit about what people on the outside think. And people applaud her for being brave and sharing the truth that so many others shy away from. They wish Sharon had opened up sooner, so they knew they weren't alone and that they were normal.

I came to the realisation in the midst of my PND that I had been using social media as a cry for help. I posted images and snippets of my life in an undercover way hoping that someone would read them and notice them as a plea for help, despite the humorous spin I tried to soften it with. That's what I do when I'm spiralling; make it funny. Distract with humour. They say if you don't laugh you'll cry, so...? But nobody heard me. I only got comparisons or likes. Nobody recognised that I was actually saying *This is what I'm dealing with and I'm struggling to handle it.*

Be careful with social media. Use it as a place to share happy times, but also use it to be kind and show empathy. Be a woke Sharon, not a twatty Sharon. And above all, remember that social media updates aren't the whole truth; they are just what the poster chooses to share, depending on how they want to be seen. Do not be judged or affected by someone else's opinion or life – that's their journey, not yours. And it's okay to show it but remember to balance and count the good alongside the bad or vice versa. Use it to share and inspire. It can be a wonderful platform if used properly. Hopefully, for most of us, our intent is never to make another person feel like shit, so before posting, think to yourself, *could what I'm about to put out there make someone feel like crap?* I urge you to think before you post, *Am I being a bit of a twat? Is this going to help or hinder someone?* Use your platform as a parent to motivate and empathise. Have a rant. Share a hack. Share the joy of a rare moment of you doing something for yourself. Show the world how content and happy your beautiful children are despite not having everything you wish you could give them, just because you are enough. Admit the consequences of a bad day. Ask for help. Just be human. Be real. And always be kind.

Money

Newborns are the cheapest variety of children. Once you've purchased all of the necessities for the early days (note: they really don't need that much despite what retailers tell you), the only thing you really have to spend money on is clothing, nappies and formula (bonus if you breastfeed). If you're lucky, you'll find you get bought a shit-load of clothing for the first six months as gifts from friends and family when the baby arrives, so really the cost of having a newborn is relatively low. Plus, there's the added benefit of something I like to call 'second-hand sibling' if you have more than one. Always save your favourite tiny clothes to pass down to the next child. That way not only do you save money, but you get to see those adorable outfits again, albeit briefly.

Ted spent his early days in sleepsuit multipacks because I think they are the epitome of baby cuteness (I cried when he grew out of them into big boy pyjamas because I knew that was the end of my sleepsuit parenting life, but also because there were no more poppers to do up –joy), but he had a fair few hand-me-down cardigans etc from H as she wasn't really a 'pink' baby girl. As a child myself, I remember wearing an awful lot of second-hand clothes passed down from my sister.

But then they grow. Babies grow faster than my pubes in winter, it's ridiculous, and as they grow, they change through the developmental stages and require toys. So many bloody toys. Your house becomes a plastic jungle, yet all they want to play with are the boxes or ride the actual dog rather than the inflatable one on wheels that Aunty Shirley bought for Christmas which takes up the entire living room. The cost of keeping these little humans creeps up month by month until they're asking for a PS5 and the latest Adidas trainers (which will only last six months because they keep growing). Household bills increase; they leave the telly and the lights on. Your internet connection gets abused, and they like to enjoy hour-long showers whilst leaving the tap running in the sink, because turning it off didn't cross their mind after using it to fill up the pool in their Barbie house. And they eat. My God do they eat. Our monthly food bill doubled every quarter of a year in the first two years of becoming parents (however, I can't deny that some of that was the necessity to buy more alcohol on the weekly shopping for us). Even at the toddler and pre-school ages, my kids already have the knack of walking into the house from an outing and going straight to the fridge for a snack. They do it without even thinking. I swear they can eat five meals a day and still inhale all the snacks in-between. It's insane how much food they can put away and still burn off the energy in one day.

Then they grow older still, and the cost of taking them on holiday increases. It's safe to say that with rapid growth increase comes rapid savings decrease.

Newborn necessities – for YOU, not for baby

Obviously, the interpretation of what you 'need' for a newborn is up to you, but I just feel the need to tell you that retailers talk shite to get your money. Yes, it's very exciting to become a parent for the first time and yes, you will obviously want to buy all the cute things that you think will make life a bit easier, and yes, as a first-time parent you have absolutely no idea what to expect, so you naturally listen to the advice from people who sell all things baby related because they must know, right? But in all honesty, it's mostly bollocks. As I said previously, babies don't require that much to keep them alive and happy. So with this in mind, I'm not going to provide you with a list of suggestions as I feel it'd be patronising your intelligence. However, I am going to go one step further. What I am going to give you will BLOW YOUR MIND. This is the ultimate list of requirements for a new mother (whether brand-new, first-time parent or knackered mother of an entire clan).

Forget about what you need for the baby for a minute. What do new mothers need for themselves? Behold the 'Newborn Mummy Hamper kit'. I have done this a few times as a baby shower gift and it has always been well received with wide eyes and nods/murmurs of "Ooh yeah" from the all-knowing, experienced and already damaged Mums present and necking gin at the back of the room…

Newborn Mummy Hamper Kit

- **3x babygrow: one in each size from tiny to 3 months,** *in case baby's weight is unexpected.*
- **A multipack of nice knickers in a bigger size than your usual**, *because pretty underwear makes you feel less like your vagina has been destroyed.*
- **Supermarket brand slimline maternity pads,** *because they don't feel like you have a wad of padding in your pants but do the same job.*
- **Tena adult pull-up pants;** *the holy grail for afterbirth bleeding.*
- **Tea tree oil** *to put in the bath to help heal stitches. You stink, but it works.*
- **Dry shampoo, hair bobbles & Femfresh wipes,** *because morning showers become a luxury.*
- **Concealer** *for under eye bags.*
- **Olive oil/almond oil** *for baby's newborn skin.*
- **Fairy non-bio washing powder and softener,** *because your washer and dryer will run daily for the foreseeable.*
- **Infacol/gripe water** *for a windy baby.*
- **Camomile tea bags for babies** *soothes and comforts in the midst of a colic meltdown (obviously read the instructions and don't just hand your newborn a brew).*
- **Biscuits,** *because it's all you'll have time to eat.*
- **Energy tablets** – *good to take out and about with you for when you're flagging on two hours sleep but can't stop.*
- **Note pad and pen,** *because your brain turns to shit, and you can't remember anything.*
- **Cheap teabags** *so you don't have to use your expensive ones on the million visitors when they come to see baby.*
- **Make-up wipes,** *because you can kiss goodbye to your evening*

skincare routine before bed.

- **A decent firming body moisturiser** *to help tighten the mum-tum if they're bothered about it.*
- **Nipple cream** – *this is pretty self-explanatory.*
- **Pile cream** – *hopefully not necessary but good to have in case you push those suckers out during the birth.*
- **Savoy cabbage** *to whack leaves in your bra which help soothe and cool (and help to dry out breastmilk if bottle feeding).*
- **Formula storage cups** *to take the exact amount when you go out, so you don't look like a twat carting a huge tin of powder about with you.*
- **Hot water bottle/reusable chill packs** *to ease swelling and soothe stitches.*
- **Perfect prep machine if formula feeding** – *literally the best contraption ever. Like a coffee machine for babies, it makes a warm bottle in under a minute so you don't have to wait for it to cool in the middle of the night when all you want to do is get back in bed.*

Disclaimer: a variety of brands are available for each product.

So, there you have it, my own tried and tested best gift for new parents. The only things which trump this collection of essentials by way of post-birth gift to a new mother would be a house cleaner every week for a month or a delivery of homemade food to last a fortnight. I have experienced and provided both of these and can confirm that when you've just had a baby, these are the God tier of congratulatory gifts.

Favourite Child

It's so true. This is the one that nobody ever admits to but exists on a daily basis. It changes depending on the daily moods and events, but generally speaking you will have a favourite child which is largely based around which one is behaving the least of a nobhead on any given day. Your favourite will change like the wind. Kids have the savage ability to reel you in with cuteness, then spit you out in an unprovoked attack on your sanity. Factors to take into consideration can include the age and needs of your child(ren), attitude, hormones, sleep (or lack thereof) and general behaviour from one day to the next. It's the one rule of silence I agree with; never to let on which of them is your favourite at any time, but make no doubt about it, favouritism exists within parenting. Likewise, they'll definitely have a favourite parent if there's two of you. Accept it and move on. It is possible to love your children unconditionally but not always like them.

Sibling rivalry

I somehow feel less of a good parent the second time around, as though I'm not sure what I'm doing, and I don't think it is just due to PND. It's as though I've lost my confidence. The pressure of splitting time so that each child gets the same amount of my attention weighs heavily on me and often brings on the mum guilt. I think I bossed it the first time, but more frequently now I feel like I'm just wading through. Am I doing enough? Are both children equally happy? Am I spreading myself thinner to provide everything I can for them both, and is the consequence of that having an effect on my own wellbeing? There's no doubt about it, mum guilt is real whether you have one child or a football team.

My eldest was thrilled when we told her she was having a sibling. She is the kind of child who craves other children for social interaction, so imagine our dismay once the youngest grew old enough that they could argue/fight/annoy each other. We thought a small age gap between them might work in our favour and they'd be so close they would forever want to be in one another's company, yet they have a very typical sibling relationship of love/hate depending on who has what and how tired they are. It's bloody soul destroying, and I spend much of my weekends refereeing, despite them still being so young. I'm already stockpiling gin for the teenage years.

Different developmental stages

As your child progresses through the newborn/baby/toddler/preschool phases, they provide you with an unpredictable pattern of development. You get settled into a routine with one thing, then WHAM, they change, and you have to reinvent the wheel again for the weeks ahead. They evolve faster than a wet fart after curry night and it's a massive headfuck to witness. They sleep for days on end at first, then they don't sleep at all. Then they sleep a bit better and gradually better still until you think you've cracked it, then teething/sleep regression hits and you're back to crying into your coffee at 04:30 every morning after three hours of broken sleep for a month.

You get into a lovely chilled little daily routine with them, then they suddenly don't like it or want to do more/less. You plan your week around said routine only for them to become a social anti-beta blocker and throw your meticulous planning out the window. It doesn't matter whether your planning includes outings, meals, sleep schedules, play time etc, there will come a time where they say 'fuck you' and put a halt to it all, then once you've cancelled your plans and changed the routine around to suit them, they actually want the old schedule back. I've learnt that although routine is important, it's also essential to take it with a chilled approach so that when they are being awkward little fuckers, you don't take it personally.

Enjoy the early days of weaning. During this time, it's likely that your baby will eat pretty much most things you put in front of them. *Broccoli? Sure Mum! Cabbage? Ooh yes please mum!* I can't stress enough, THIS DOES NOT LAST, and when it changes, be prepared for a fight. Arm yourself with knowledge and bribery to explain to a toddler why vegetables are so important. Home in on their likes, "Well, Spiderman eats spinach, that's how he gets his sticky web..", because they will literally try anything to get out of eating something they don't want to. Keep your calm. Don't lose your shit like I have many a time, "You ate fucking carrots yesterday and liked them", and do not give in. It's your job to instil the values of nutrition into them from an early age. Don't get me wrong, I'm all for an easy fish fingers or nuggets bang-in-the-oven tea, but in moderation. From my experience, the more frequent those meals become, the more stubborn the rejection is when you place a stir fry in front of them. Oh, and don't forget to serve the beverage in the right cup. God forbid you give a toddler or pre-schooler the wrong fucking cup with their food.

Potty training can absolutely fuck off. I hate it; surprise behind-the-couch poos, wet patches on the carpet, multipacks of sodden underwear, ruined shoes which cost a fortune for such tiny feet, a bathroom that resembles the men's toilet at the club I used to frequent in my teens and odours of shit floating about in every room. It stresses me out, but it is one of those rites of passage every parent has to manoeuvre their way through. I recommend 'well done' stickers for them and a lot of gin for you.

Speech and language development is probably my favourite part of watching my kids grow. Aside from the fact that Harriet once could not make a sound, yet now she does not shut up from the moment she wakes up to the minute she falls asleep, I love the things that come out of children's mouths. You never know what's coming. Their filters are more inadequate than mine, but they have an excuse for it. Kids are brutal in their honesty and air their views without the ability to mince their words. They tell it exactly like it is. From those first babbles, to the use of conjunctions to string longer sentences together. It makes me smile to think how clever they are. Then they don't stop talking and I don't smile as much. They become loud and relentless with their vocals and learn how to answer back and repeat what you say out of context to strangers. Harriet once told a neighbour to "Fog off" as she casually strolled past them as they were watering their front garden. She was holding my hand and smiling sweetly. I assume it was a mix of *Bog off* and *Fuck off*. She also went through a stage of muttering "Fugging egg" under her breath when she didn't get her way as a toddler. They will definitely get you into trouble and embarrass you with their words on more than one occasion. That said, they also come out with some absolute belters of words when they can't verbalise the correct pronunciation. Always write them down as they happen to remind yourself (and them) one day when they're older, because those are the types of moments that you'll miss when you look back and can't remember.

Last, but not least on the list of expectation vs. reality, is sibling rivalry. You have that beautiful baby, and you decide you want another one. Whether it's immediately or further down the line, it doesn't matter, you make the decision based upon an image of two or more children, hand in hand, looking out for one another and always being there in childhood memories. You hope that they will always be close and have each other's backs, but what you don't visualise is the early battle of strong wills and nasty words between them, however harmless. You don't imagine them kicking the shit out of each other on a Sunday morning whilst rolling around on your couch cushions which they were using to build a fort with peacefully together ten seconds ago. You don't envision the intentional trip up by one of them as the other runs past. You don't think of the bickering and squabbling over toys to the point of tears, or the fact that neither of them want to share you with the other which causes your thighs to cramp as you balance one on each knee, despite their weight, just to stop an argument. They can be utter bastards to each other. Then you turn your back and find them cuddled together or sharing something moments later. Siblings are brilliant. I think every parent would say they hope that the peaceful and 'as one' nature of a sibling relationship is maintained through to adulthood, but as many of us will have seen, it isn't always the case. Blood isn't always thicker than water, but whilst they're still small, fill their heads with so much love for one another and just hope that the bond is strong enough to last.

So to summarise this chapter, let me round up the key information that I have learnt about myself and about children since become a parent:

1. I have an untapped patience resource which I didn't know existed until I had children.
2. Toddlers are savage, sneaky, and emotionally unstable.
3. There is nothing worse than being ill but still having to parent.
4. The smell of my babies after bathing is the best smell ever.
5. Single parents deserve medals.
6. Silence is suspicious.
7. There is an art to 'cleaning' the parts of the house that people might see with a packet of baby wipes, which once mastered brings me great smugness and satisfaction.
8. Every parent is winging it.
9. Work is a welcome break from reality.
10. I will rarely get to eat a meal without sharing my food for the next few years.
11. I struggle to remember the feeling I got from life before kids now, but although I miss aspects of it, I wouldn't change being a mum to my two for anything.
12. There are times when I want to stay up late because it is the only time I will get to myself, but 8 p.m. bedtime is the new 11 p.m. bedtime. I will thank myself for it the following day.
13. There's no point crying over spilt Cheerios, unless they are soggy and trodden into carpet.

9.

Closure

Final words

So there you have it, parents, my unfiltered view on becoming 'Mum'. I've written openly and honestly about my own experiences and the sometimes-unavoidable aspects of parenting; words and advice which I found lacking in those early days of 'What the holy hell has happened to my life'. It won't be the same for everyone. Different people will have different journeys, but if what I have admitted to can help just one person make light of the madness of having children and the trip that follows, then my job here is done.

My children are my everything. My little family is my bubble. Every night, I look at Harriet in awe of her beauty and her innocence. I gaze at Ted and know he made me stronger than I ever thought I could be. I hold my husband's hand tight in the knowledge that whatever happens we will overcome it together. Collectively, those three humans are the reason I have lost a degree of my sanity but the reason I live and breathe. Every family has dysfunction; there is no such thing as normal and for that we are no exception. Every day, I am learning to choose my battles and go with the flow. Winging it is a common verb in my vocabulary. Before parenthood, I never ever expected to be this person. I didn't realise how many things you could feel at once and how much I would miss myself sometimes, but at the same time, I also didn't realise how proud I would be of myself.

During the writing of this book, we lost Sean, one of our best friends, to cancer at the age of 34. It knocked me sideways and buried my soul a little deeper into the black hole that was already consuming me, but it was also the thing that built me back up. Loss and grief made me realise that life is far too short and unpredictable to be spent on giving a fuck what other people think. Strength is an achievement. Spreading laughter and making people smile was one of his best qualities on top of being an absolutely awesome father. We entered the parenting journey six months apart and shared so many WTF moments, wondering why we didn't know half the shit that came with it beforehand, so when I took a break from writing during his illness, it was the stories and videos of our kids that we had shared and laughed at which helped me to pull myself back to it.

I hope you feel enlightened and not at all offended by my insight.

If you're a parent-to-be with Number One on the way, I hope you've found my words useful and not too terrifyingly honest.

And if you've already been there and done that, then I hope your kids gave you enough quiet time to read and that somewhere within my words you related to something.

My mum always taught me that "Honesty is the best policy". I couldn't agree more.

Now, where's the gin?

Cheers, motherfuckers – we are all legends.

Acknowledgements

Because manners are very important

Firstly, I would like to thank my children, without whom I would not have had the content to spew my thoughts onto page. I love you both unconditionally and more than any words could say. You drive me mad (literally) and are the reason I enjoy gin so much, but I wouldn't have my world without you. Thank you for teaching me how to be a Mum – I hope I have lived up to your expectations.

Secondly, I need to thank Ste my long-suffering husband. Thank you for standing by me. Thank you for literally holding me up from the floor in my lowest moments. Thank you for trying to understand and for your patience. Thank you for supporting me and making me laugh. Thank you for our two beautiful, albeit frequently irritating children.

A huge thank you goes to my close friends and employers, The Smiths who took a chance on a low paid teaching assistant and gave me the job of my dreams and with that, the confidence to do more and reach high. From watching your success and celebrating alongside you, you gave me inspiration to push myself further. Not only that, but you've been a vital source of experienced parent friends who have shared my WTF moments alongside your own. Thank you also for introducing me to posh gin.

Another thank you goes to Mel at Moment of Proof for her kindness and enthusiasm whilst editing my grammar and vocabulary. Thank you to Jen at Fuzzy Flamingo for your professional typesetting skills and helping me to bring the finished product together, and to Shammy Walton for your talented hand on designing the cover. I owe each of you a massive cocktail.

Also, a big shout out goes to Jose Jackson for providing me with the brews, chat, courage and the head space which I needed in order to share this.

Lastly, to my friends and family – thank you all. Thanks for your support and love which has got me through the tough bits. To my girls (you know who you are), you're next… hurry up please.

Love, peace and a magnum of prosecco!

H xxx

www.ingramcontent.com/pod-product-compliance
Lightning Source LLC
Chambersburg PA
CBHW031646170726
47990CB00019B/2613